Reviews For:

Hope for the Holidays

Andrew Lay leads us into Advent/Christmas and, creatively listening to the old, familiar texts, finds fresh meaning for today's Christians. Lay restores the holy to the holidays in this fine presentation of the blessing of the Incarnation.

—**Bishop Will Willimon**, Professor of *the Practice of Christian Ministry, Duke Divinity School*, author of *Accidental Preacher: A Memoir*.

***

Hope for the Holidays offers hope for Advent and common days. It is very interesting, informative, and inspirational. In examining John the Baptist, Joseph, Mary, the Shepherds, and Wise Men, we are led to see that God is involved in the lives of ordinary people in extraordinary ways. The author has a unique ability to make real these ancient characters of our faith. We see and feel their struggles for faith in dark moments. We see how their attempts to make sense of life reflect our own, and we come to understand that God is with us as well. If God could bless and use them, why

i

not us? If God gave hope then, why not now? I give thanks for the privilege of having my faith renewed through this remarkable writing and heartily commend it to you.

—**Bishop Richard Looney**, Retired Bishop of *The United Methodist Church.*

***

In this well written book, Andrew Lay fleshes out John the Baptist, Joseph, Mary, Isaiah and the Shepherds, the Wise Men as heralds of hope. As if arriving at Bethlehem's manger, these explorations culminate, in the Epilogue, in the Word Made Flesh to which these heralds point. All along, Lay invites his readers to narrate their own lives in light of the Christmas hope to which its first celebrants pointed. Questions at the end of each chapter help readers make the connection between the biblical story and their own, and also make the book useful for group or individual use. There are many Advent studies and devotional volumes available, but Lay leads us by a fresh, thoughtful, and pastoral route to the heart of the Christmas hope. I strongly commend *Hope for the Holidays* to all who, like the Wise Men themselves, wish to "return by another way," to their lives after the holidays are over; to lives filled with the hope that enfleshed Word brings daily.

—**William McDonald**, Professor of *Religion, Chair - Religion and Philosophy*, Associate Dean - *Humanities & Fine Arts, Tennessee Wesleyan University*.

***

In these troubled and bewildering times, we yearn for an enduring hope that sustains us and pulls us toward a promising future. As Andrew Lay reminds us, that enduring hope is found in the Christmas Story as God works through ordinary people to accomplish the divine purposes. The author introduces us anew to the characters in the Christmas Story; and through their responses to God's revelation, our hope is renewed, and our faith is strengthened. This engaging book is an excellent resource for individuals and groups who long for "hope for the holiday" and beyond.

—**Bishop Kenneth L. Carder**, Williams Distinguished Professor Emeritus of *the Practice of Christian Ministry, Duke Divinity School*.

***

Finding hope may be the first and most basic task of faith. In Hope for the Holidays, Andrew Lay peels back the layers of the Christmas story to help us discover a wellspring of unending hope in a most unlikely place. If you're having trouble finding hope these days, my advice is to start your search by finding a copy of Hope for the Holidays.

—**Rev. Wil Cantrell,** *Concord United Methodist Church, Knoxville, TN.*

HOPE FOR THE HOLIDAYS

Exploring the Message of Hope
In the Christmas Story

ANDREW CURTIS LAY

What is Christmas?
It is tenderness for the past,
courage for the present,
hope for the future.
– Agnes M. Pharo

Christmas is not
a story of hope.
It is hope.
–Craig D. Lounsbrough

To my wife Ally –

my best friend and the love of my life

ACKNOWLEDGEMENTS

I want to thank all the folks at Kharis Publishing who helped, supported, and encouraged me throughout this process. I am grateful to James Clement, the acquisitions and operations lead, who stayed in contact with me and guided this process. To my editor Karen Corinne Herceg and her excellent editorial work. She worked diligently to elevate, critique, and enhance my writings. To the graphics team who worked to make this book eye-catching, thank you.

I am grateful to all the people at Keith Memorial United Methodist Church for their support and encouragement. It is an honor to serve as one of your pastors, and I'm so glad I get to join you all in ministry – I love you all. I also want to thank our senior pastor, David Graybeal for all the ways that he has inspired and encouraged me during this project. Thank you for being my trusted colleague, mentor, and friend.

I'm grateful to my parents who have always been my biggest fans. Mom and Dad, you two are the greatest examples of how to live out the Christian faith. Thank you for making me the person I am today. I want to thank the rest of my family – I am so glad I get to share the holidays and the special times in my life with you all of you. To my friends – each of you means so much to me. Thanks for all the memories we have made, eating wings, watching hockey, and sharing life together.

Finally, I want to thank my wife, Ally, for her support. I have spent countless hours in meetings, answering emails, writing sermons, and working on this book. Thank you for putting up with all of this. Thank you for reading every draft of this book and never complaining. I am so glad to have you by my side through all of life's twists and turns. I couldn't do this without you.

CONTENTS

INTRODUCTION

Hope for the Holidays is more than just a catchy phrase that you might find in a Hallmark greeting or the possible title of a cheesy Lifetime movie. Hope is a profound and necessary thing for us to experience, and it is often the most prevalent during the season of Christmas. This book discusses the message of hope that we find in throughout the Christmas story, as we celebrate Jesus' birth and anticipate his second coming.

This message of hope is something that we desperately need. There are times when we feel like we are surrounded by experiences of pain, loss, and suffering. In the midst of these times, it can be hard to see any good. During much of 2020 and 2021, we found ourselves in the midst of a global pandemic. On the news we witness numerous accounts of violence and racism. We hear about school shootings and acts of terrorism. And we also experience times in our own lives that are difficult and challenging. During these trying moments in life, it can be hard to find the hope that is present in our lives. The Christmas season is a time that is full and ripe with hope.

My wife, Ally, and I celebrated our first Christmas together in the year 2020. It was an unusual first year of marriage because of the coronavirus pandemic. We had to limit the number of people who attended our wedding to ten; we weren't able to go on a honeymoon; and we were largely confined to our home. At the end of October, Ally said, "Hey, why don't we go ahead and put up our Christmas tree early? It's been a hard year, and I just need to experience the Christmas season a little bit sooner this year."

So, that is exactly what we did. I have to say that I enjoyed our Christmas decorations more this year than I had since I was a young child. Despite dealing with the strange circumstances that come with a pandemic, Ally and I we were able to find a deeper sense of love and appreciation for one another. We were able to spend a lot of quality time together. We were able to experience the hope of Christmas in a new and different way. One thing is clear: Christmas 2020 will be one that we will never forget.

In the Christmas season, we find hope knowing that Christ has come to dwell among us as Emmanuel, which means "God with us." That is what we celebrate at Christmas – "the Incarnation" – when Jesus came in the flesh to dwell among us, and we hold on to the hope that Christ will come again to make all things new. This understanding is what gives us hope knowing that the brokenness and pain that exist in our world will one day be made right. We don't have to fend for ourselves. We are not hopeless. We are not alone. God is with us.

In this book, we will explore the ways we can experience hope for the holidays. In each chapter, we will look at the different characters in the Christmas story and how they offer us messages of hope to us in our own lives. In Chapter One, we will focus on John the Baptist's message concerning the hope of salvation. In Chapter Two, we will turn to the story of Joseph and the hope that he finds in the angel's message about the birth of Emmanuel. In Chapter Three, we will look at the hope for justice that Mary expresses in her song, The Magnificat. In Chapter Four, we will explore the hope that is proclaimed to the shepherds about the birth of the Christ Child. In Chapter Five, we will address the hope that is fulfilled through the Wise Men who visited Jesus. In the Epilogue, we will revisit the hope that is made flesh in the Incarnation of Jesus who dwells among us.

My hope is that you will read this book during the season of Advent and that you will encounter this story in a fresh and new way. As you read, may you explore this message of hope in the Christmas story, but may you also explore the message of hope in your own life as well. May you be filled with God's message of hope as your journey to Christmas.

Andrew Curtis Lay.

CHAPTER ONE

JOHN THE BAPTIST
HOPE OF SALVATION

A voice cries out: "In the wilderness prepare the way of the Lord, make straight in the desert a highway for our God."

—Isaiah 40:3

As the people were filled with expectation, and all were questioning in their hearts concerning John, whether he might be the Messiah, John answered all of them by saying, "I baptize you with water; but one who is more powerful than I is coming; I am not worthy to untie the thong of his sandals. He will baptize you with the Holy Spirit and fire. His winnowing fork is in his hand, to clear his threshing floor and to gather the wheat into his granary; but the chaff he will burn with unquenchable fire."

—Luke 3:15-17

During the season of Christmas, we are invited to receive a message that is focused on the hope, peace, joy, and love of Christ. It is a special season when we are called to remember the Christ who came to us at Christmas and anticipate Christ's second coming. For many, Christmas is a time when we experience hope in circumstances that might seem hopeless.

As we look around at our world, we see examples of racism, violence, and injustice, and we are reminded of our need for a Savior to come into the world and right all of our wrongs. We can turn on CNN or listen to NPR and find examples of injustice and oppression in the United States of America and around the world. We witness tragic and horrific events almost daily. I can think of several recent examples.

On February 14, 2018, a gunman entered Marjory Stoneman Douglas High School in Parkland, Florida. The shooter, a 19-year-old man, opened fire with a semi-automatic rifle, killing 17 people. This tragic event marked the deadliest high school shooting in United States history.

On May 25, 2020, the world was shocked by the murder of George Floyd in Minneapolis, Minnesota. George Floyd was accused of buying cigarettes with a counterfeit $20 bill. In response to the call, three police officers pinned Floyd down for 8 minutes and 46 seconds. One of these officers had his knee lodged against Floyd's throat which cut off his air supply, causing his death.

On January 6, 2021, as the House and Senate were voting to certify the results of our 2020 Presidential Election, we witnessed throngs of people storm past the police and into the United States Capitol Building.

They tussled with officers in full riot gear, broke into the chambers, and entered governmental offices. They carried Confederate flags and were adorned with Nazi symbols. Five people died because of this domestic terrorist attack.

We are in need of a Savior. We need Christ to bring hope to the world. In our pain and suffering, we find hope in the coming of Christ. In the message of Jesus' birth, we receive, as the Christmas hymn "O Holy Night" says:

> *A thrill of hope the weary world rejoices.*
> *For yonder breaks a new and glorious morn.*

No matter how grim our world might seem, we can still experience the hope that comes at Christmas. Hope is a powerful thing, and we need it now more than ever. In this chapter, we will explore John the Baptist's message concerning the hope of salvation in Christ.

I've always been fascinated with John the Baptist, because he seems like such a strange and bizarre character. The Gospels of Matthew and Mark both describe John the Baptist as a rugged and unkempt wild man, wearing clothing of camel's hair with a leather belt around his waist. We are told that he eats locusts and wild honey. I imagine him looking similar to Grizzly Adams, the frontier woodsman who is completely one with nature. He is clearly an ascetic who lived out in the desert and denied himself of the luxuries of city living. Matthew and Mark's Gospels help paint us a vivid picture in our minds of how John the Baptist might have looked and acted.

The Gospels of Luke and John, however, omit these strange and bizarre little details about John the Baptist's appearance and diet. In Luke's and John's Gospels, there is no mention of the camel hair clothing or the leather belt. There is no word about eating locusts or wild honey. Instead, the emphasis is placed, not on what John looks like, but on what he says. The focus is on his message. This is actually a good thing, because Luke' sand John's Gospels force us to focus more on the substance of John the Baptist's message which is a message of hope.

John's Prophetic Message

John the Baptist speaks as a prophet. He speaks as God's mouthpiece, joining the ranks of the Old Testament prophets: Isaiah, Jeremiah, Ezekiel, and Elijah. In fact, he has been described as the last of the Old Testament prophets and the first of the New Testament prophets.

In the Gospel of John, the crowds even ask John the Baptist if he *is* the prophet Elijah. This is an interesting question considering Elijah had been spared the pain of death and was raised up to heaven *(see John 1:21)*. But John is quick to tell the crowds that he is not Elijah, or the Messiah for that matter. Instead, he comes to speak the word of God with a voice calling in the wilderness, proclaiming a baptism of repentance for the forgiveness of sins. In the wilderness, John quotes the prophet Isaiah:

> *A voice cries out:*
> *"In the wilderness prepare the way of the Lord,*
> *make straight in the desert a highway for our God."*
> —Isaiah 40:3

John's message is actually quite simple. John essentially says, "Prepare yourselves. The Messiah is coming, and you need to be ready. Come, repent, and be baptized." John works to prepare humanity for the coming of the Messiah. John preaches to the masses, and he invites them to be baptized in the Jordan River in order to prepare their hearts for the One who is to come.

Preparation is an important aspect of celebrating the Christmas season. There is a lot that needs to be done. We have to shop and buy gifts. We attend Christmas parties. We visit family. We cook food. We do all of these things and more. There is so much that needs to be done in order to celebrate Christmas, but John the Baptist prepares us in a deeper way. John works to introduce the character of Jesus and prepares us for his coming.

People from Jerusalem, Judea, and all over the Jordan Valley go out into the desert to see and hear John. He preaches, he calls for repentance, and he even listens to your confessions. It's not surprising that all these people are willing to travel to the desert, in the middle of nowhere, to listen to this preacher.

There's something special about going off to some stranger in the desert to tell your confession and to be baptized. People are more likely to tell their deepest darkest secrets to complete strangers instead of their closest friends. John the Baptist is not somebody you're going to run into at the grocery store. He's not somebody your friends are going to know. He's not somebody who will go around spreading all your secrets.

Perhaps this was the first opportunity for the people in Jerusalem, Judea, and the Jordan Valley to worship in a place where they didn't feel judged. This was a place that was safe from the stares and glares of the social elite. He gives the people a renewed sense of hope.

What is so interesting about this message, however, is that it isn't offered by any of the important leaders of the day. It isn't proclaimed by any of the rulers in the Roman government. It isn't from the supreme ruler of the Roman Empire, Tiberius Claudius Caesar Augustus. It isn't from Pontius Pilate, the governor of Judea. It isn't from King Herod, the Jewish leader in charge of Galilee. Or his brother Philip who ruled over Trachonitis and Iturea. Or from Lysanius who ruled Abilene. Nor is it from any of the leaders of the Jewish community. It isn't from the high priest Annas or Caiaphas.

Instead, we hear about the coming Messiah – who will challenge the existing power structure and turn it on its head – from none other than John the Baptist, the relative of Jesus. John the Baptist's voice rises above all the political powers of his day. This message comes from the most unexpected place and from the most unexpected person. As Marvin McMickle says:

> *Our world is fascinated with the rich and famous and powerful, but among them we will not necessarily find persons at work with God... Instead, God chose to go to work radically among the weak, the lowly, and the despised. The church has a message that will not be heard from the White House or on CNN – that is, to repent. The just society that we desire cannot be achieved by an act of Congress or a ruling by the U.S. Supreme Court. The church must*

declare its message of repentance for the forgiveness of sins and the call to transformation.[1]

Ultimately, one of the political powers will seek revenge against John the Baptist for his prophetic voice. Herod Antipas feared John the Baptist and his message about the coming Messiah. Herod imprisons and beheads John for speaking out against Herod's decision to marry Herodias, his brother Philip's wife. As Mark's Gospel states:

For John had been telling Herod,
"It is not lawful for you to have your brother's wife."
—Mark 6:18

John the Baptist prepares the way for the Lord. He made way for Jesus' birth. He baptized Jesus before he began his ministry. He preached a message of repentance in preparation for Jesus' forthcoming judgement. John also prepares Jesus for his death. John is arrested before Jesus is arrested. John is imprisoned before Jesus is imprisoned. John is beheaded before Jesus is crucified. Yet again, one last time, John prepares the way for the Lord.

The Promised Messiah

John points us to Jesus, not as a cute little baby laying in a manger. No, John points to a different kind of Jesus. John points to the Jesus who told his disciples, "deny yourself, take up your cross and follow me." John points to the Jesus who broke down the social barriers that divided people, who touched lepers, and ate with sinners and tax collectors. John points to the Jesus who forgave the unforgiveable and loved the unlovable.

In the remote wilderness in the region of Jordan, John the Baptist tells us about the coming Christ who will give humanity a hopeful future. And this coming Messiah will confront the problems that plague our world. John the Baptist says:

> *Every valley shall be filled, and every mountain and hill shall be made low, and the crooked shall be made straight, and the rough ways made smooth; and all flesh shall see the salvation of God.*
> —Luke 3:5, 6

In other words, Jesus will come and even the playing field. Jesus will come and right every wrong. This is a message of hope that we desperately need. We need Jesus to come into our lives and address the white privilege and systemic racism that plagues our society.

We need Jesus to come into our lives and confront the systems of injustice and oppression that run rampant in our communities. We need Jesus to come into our lives to exalt the lowly and humble the proud. We need Jesus to come into our lives and turn things on its head and shake us up. And this is exactly what Jesus does, when we allow him to work in our lives.

Transformation is a difficult thing to enter into, especially when you find yourself in a place of power. But John reminds us that it doesn't matter who your mother and daddy are. It doesn't matter if you are a Roman citizen. It doesn't matter if you are a Pharisee. It doesn't matter if you are descendent of Abraham. It doesn't matter if you are an American. John says:

Bear fruits worthy of repentance. Do not begin to say to yourselves, "We have Abraham as our ancestor"; for I tell you, God is able from these stones to raise up children to Abraham.
—Luke 3:8

John really lays into the crowd. John does not try to sugar coat the message of who Jesus is. He lets us know that our actions and the things that we do truly matter, saying:

Even now the ax is lying at the root of the trees; every tree therefore that does not bear good fruit is cut down and thrown into the fire.
—Luke 3:9

John the Baptist essentially tells the crowd that if they want to be a part of this new movement, then they are going to have to change some things. John invites them into a new way of life through repentance and baptism. The crowd hears John's harsh condemnation, and they seem to respond out of a sense of hopelessness.

In Luke 3:10, you can almost hear their desperation as they ask, "What then should we do?" The crowd is confronted with the brokenness that is rampant in their lives, and they are seeking an answer from John the Baptist: What then should we do?

Fruits of Repentance

In Luke 3:11-14, John speaks of having two coats and giving away one. The same applies to extra food. The tax collectors challenge this and ask what they should do. John tells them not to collect more than what the law allows. Then soldiers show up and ask what they should do. John advises them not to cheat, harass or blackmail anyone and to be satisfied with their salaries.

Interestingly, enough, this monk-like wild man doesn't tell the crowd that they too must turn their backs on their ways of life and come follow him in the desert. He doesn't tell them that they have to be like him and live out in the wilderness as a recluse.

Instead, John tells the crowd to work within their own lives, jobs, and circumstances. Tax collectors are called to bear good fruit *as* tax collectors. Soldiers are called to bear good fruit *as* soldiers. John tells us to simply do the right thing; to bear fruits worthy of repentance; to right our wrongs; to treat others with love, respect, and fairness; to do good works in our daily lives.

It is the same for us. We are called to live out our vocations – as parents, doctors, waiters, teachers, students, and as Christians. We are called to bear good fruit within our own situations in life. So, how can you go out into the world and bear fruits worthy of repentance? What are the wrongs that you need to right in your own life? Who have you harmed and sinned against? Where have you failed to live the life that Christ is calling you to live?

As Christians, we know that we cannot earn our salvation by simply bearing good fruit. We believe that we are saved by faith alone, apart from good works. But we also believe that repentance is a necessary response in our faith as we accept the justifying grace of Jesus Christ. Repentance opens up possibilities for us to live out the Christian life and to bear good fruit into the world.

The Greek word for "repentance" is the word *metanoia* which literally means "afterthought." Repentance is a change of mind about something that you previously believed.[2] True repentance is a complete transformation in how you think, what you believe, and how you live out your life. In his sermon "Justification by Faith," John Wesley, the founder of the Methodist Movement, writes:

> *Thus "through the offence of one" all are dead, dead to God, dead in sin, dwelling in a corruptible, mortal body, shortly to be dissolved, and under the sentence of death eternal.[3]*

According to Wesley, humans are corrupt, and they are found dead in their sin. In other words, sin separates humankind from God. Human beings are born into original sin which damages their relationship with God, and repentance is the way for humans to turn away from their sin and find God's divine grace. Repentance invites us to acknowledge our sin, change direction, and embrace Christ.

Wesley preached about the three graces that make up his "Order of Salvation." Prevenient grace is the grace that goes before everything else. Wesley believed that every human being was capable of some good and, therefore, capable of salvation. Prevenient grace is preparation for humans to receive justification. Looking back on life, one can see how God was present in their life through prevenient grace.

Justification or justifying grace is the forgiveness of our sins and our acceptance with God. In other words, justifying grace is a pardon for one's sin. Christians are justified through the blood of Jesus Christ. Believers are justified by faith alone in Jesus

Christ, and faith is the only condition of justification. Repentance is an important part of the process of justification.

Sanctification is when one is "born again" through the Spirit. The goal of sanctification is to become more like Christ. Entire sanctification does not mean that one is free from temptation or mistakes, but it relates to experiencing the fullness of the Spirit in love.

According to Wesley, sanctification should also be partnered with works of piety, such as prayer and Bible study. Final Sanctification relates to those who are resurrected into a new level of reality. Final Sanctification means that one's scars are liberated, and this process will take place in heaven.

In his message, John the Baptist invites us to enter into prevenient, justifying, and sanctifying grace. He invites us to enter into this process of becoming holy as God is holy. He invites us to show the world that we have changed through the way that we act. It's not just about feeling sorry for what we've done wrong, but it is about making a change in our lives. And that change is expressed through our actions. It is expressed in the way that we live our lives.

Invitation of Hope

I find it interested that in this harsh message from John there is still an invitation. There is room for everyone to repent and to change. Everyone is invited. Everyone can belong. Everyone can experience the good news of the coming Messiah. All of this can happen all because of the repentance that we can find in

Christ. John the Baptist tells us that it's time to change.

In this message, we receive hope. We have hope for a better future. We have hope for a second and a third and a fourth chance. We have the opportunity to address the conditions of our hearts and experience the hope of salvation. As the retired United Methodist Bishop Will Willimon says:

> *The prophets speak of that day when God will at last come to redeem a lost and fallen world. The world, as it is, is not the world that God intended when God began creating the world. So the prophets preach fierce judgment against our unrighteousness... In order to prepare ourselves for the advent of the Christ, we must face God's judgment against us. God loves us enough not to leave us to our own devices. God comes to us, reveals the truth to us, and enables us to bear the truth in order that we might be able to receive the Christ who comes to redeem us.[4]*

One Sunday morning, I had just finished preaching my sermon for the day. It had been a particularly long morning, probably because I wasn't entirely thrilled with how my sermon had turned out. For whatever reason, I just felt like my sermon didn't really connect with the congregation.

But following the service, one of my church members approached me with a serious look on her face. I immediately began to think that something was wrong. This woman was in her mid-forties and had only recently started coming to the church. My initial thought was that I had said something in my sermon that had offended her.

I was shocked, however, when she told me that my sermon had actually made a positive impact on her. (This goes to show that God can work even in the midst of a terrible sermon, which is good news for me.) "Your sermon this morning really made me think about my life and my faith journey," she said, "And I'm just not sure if I'm a Christian. What do I need to do to be saved?"

Now, I have to admit that I did not answer this question in the same way that John the Baptist had talked to the crowd. I didn't call her a viper. I didn't tell her that an ax was waiting to chop her down if she didn't bear good fruit.

Instead, we sat down in one of the pews in the sanctuary, and we had a conversation. We talked about God's grace and love. We talked about what she was feeling and experiencing. We talked about what it means to be a Christian. And toward the end of our conversation, she told me that this was the first time anyone had ever really explained Christianity to her, and that she was ready to give her life over to Christ. So, she did just that. We prayed together, and she left church that morning different than how she came in. She left that morning as a changed person. As the theologian Kathy Beach-Verhey says:

> The word of hope to those in the wilderness is that all will be made new. The rough places will be smooth, and the crooked shall be made straight. The wilderness is not only a place where we are jerked from our comfort zones and challenged to hear God's word, but also the place where the trouble, the hurting, the alienated, the angry, and the forlorn may hear a word of hope and renewal and discover the possibility for rebirth and change.[5]

Out of the desert, John the Baptist preaches on the importance of repentance. He is so convincing that the crowd starts to wonder if maybe John, himself, is the Messiah. But John is quick to correct them. John says:

> *I baptize you with water; but one who is more powerful than I is coming; I am not worthy to untie the thong of his sandals. He will baptize you with the Holy Spirit and fire. His winnowing fork is in his hand, to clear his threshing floor and to gather the wheat into his granary; but the chaff he will burn with unquenchable fire.*
>
> —Luke 3:16, 17

John tells us that Christ is coming, and we must change. John the Baptist is preparing us for the coming Messiah. May you experience the hope of salvation.

God of hope, we thank you for the opportunities that we have to take stock of our own lives and to look at the condition of our own hearts. Help us to address the ways in which we might need to change and turn away from the things that are holding us back from you. May we strive to grow in our faith so that we can better love you and love our neighbors. And may you continue to work on our hearts as we prepare for the coming of your Son at Christmas. We thank you for the continued hope that we find in your unconditional love and grace. May we embrace your gift of life in our hearts. Amen.

Reflection Questions

1. John the Baptist was a voice crying out in the wilderness: "Prepare the way for the Lord." What are some ways that you prepare for Christmas? What are some of the traditions that you and your family celebrate?

2. How have you experienced the need for the hope of salvation in your own life? How might you share a message of hope with those who feel hopeless?

3. From the wilderness, John preaches about the hope of salvation. Have you ever experienced a time in your life when you were in the wilderness and needed a word of hope? How did you grow from coming out of that experience?

4. John tells the crowd to prepare for the coming of the Lord by bearing "fruits worthy of repentance." How have you experienced repentance that led to a change of attitude or heart in your own life?

5. John invites the crowd, the tax collectors, and the soldiers to re-examine and reshape their daily lives. How might the Lord be calling you to re-examine and reshape your life? What are some specific things that you can do to bear fruits of repentance in your life?

CHAPTER TWO

JOSEPH
HOPE FOR EMMANUEL

*Therefore the Lord himself will give you a sign.
Look, the young woman is with child and shall
bear a son, and shall name him Immanuel.*
                                            —Isaiah 7:14

*An angel of the Lord appeared to him in a
dream and said, "Joseph, son of David, do not be
afraid to take Mary as your wife, for the child
conceived in her is from the Holy Spirit. She will
bear a son, and you are to name him Jesus, for
he will save his people from their sins."*
                                            —Matthew 1:20b, 21

During the Christmas season, a lot of attention is given to Mary, the mother of Jesus, and we tend to gloss over poor Joseph the carpenter. Mary is celebrated for her obedience and courage in the midst of an unexpected pregnancy; however, Joseph's role in the story of the birth of Jesusis also incredibly important. Joseph finds himself in an impossible situation, and he, like Mary, responds with obedience and courage. In this chapter, we are looking at Joseph and the hope that he finds in the angel's message about the birth of Emmanuel.

A Hopeful Beginning

I proposed to my wife, Ally, at the University of Tennessee Gardens on May 24, 2019. We were surrounded by hydrangeas, roses, dogwoods, and lilies. It was a beautiful setting. I got down on one knee and said, "281 years ago, on May 24, 1738, John Wesley went to a Moravian meeting in Aldersgate. There he heard Martin Luther's Preface to the Romans. Wesley wrote in his journal, 'I felt my heart strangely warmed.' Ally, you have strangely warmed my heart. So, will you marry me?"

Despite this extremely nerdy proposal, Ally actually said yes. We were so excited to start our lives together. I could not stop smiling, and Ally could not stop shedding happy tears. We were full of hope as we looked forward to our future together with one another.

I imagine Mary and Joseph's engagement started off with a similar sense of excitement and hope. Mary and Joseph seem like a young couple who are excited to start their lives with one another. There is such promise for a bright future as they look forward to their wedding day.

After all, this is a special time in any couple's relationship. You anticipate sharing your life with your future spouse, having children, and growing old together. It is an exciting time as you anticipate what the future might hold. For Mary and Joseph, however, their hope and excitement must have turned to anxiety and fear, as they receive news of an unexpected child that will soon come into their lives.

Of course, we know that newborn babies are the greatest joy in the world. But to parents who are not prepared, an unexpected baby might seem more like an intrusion. Caring for an infant is a lot of responsibility. It involves changing diapers, fixing bottles, and getting up in the middle of the night to rock the baby back to sleep. It completely changes your world.

But to make matters worse, there is a deeper problem going on. Not only is Mary faced with a surprise pregnancy, but her fiancé Joseph isn't the father. Suddenly this fairy tale image of this couple living happily ever after is starting to look more like an episode of reality TV. I can almost hear Maury Povich say, *The DNA results have come back, and Joseph, you are not the father.*

The truth is Mary had not been unfaithful to Joseph. She had not committed adultery. In fact, she was personally dealing with the confusing news that she was pregnant. And to complicate things even more, she was also a virgin who was with child from the Holy Spirit. As Matthew's Gospel says:

Now the birth of Jesus the Messiah took place in this way. When his mother Mary had been engaged to Joseph, but before they lived together, she was found to be with child from the Holy Spirit.
—Matthew 1:18

Joseph is a humble carpenter and Mary is a typical young woman. Both Mary and Joseph are ordinary people who find themselves dealing with the most extraordinary circumstances. Their mundane lives have now become complicated, but it seems like God is at work. God is doing something in the midst of the chaos and confusion.

Unexpected Interruptions

Sometimes life can throw us for a loop; although, maybe not quite as bad as the one that life threw Mary and Joseph. Out of the blue, we receive news that completely changes the trajectory of our lives – both good and bad. Learning that your cancer is no longer in remission. Finding out that a loved one has passed away. Or maybe accepting a new job on the other side of the country, requiring you to uproot your family and move away from all that is familiar. And yes, maybe even the news of an unexpected pregnancy.

Life can sometimes seem chaotic and unpredictable. These moments in life are often called "liminal." In her book *How to Lead When You Don't Know Where You're Going*, Susan Beaumont defines liminality by writing:

> *Liminality refers to a quality of ambiguity or disorientation that occurs during transition, when a person or group of people is in between something that has ended and something else that is not yet ready to begin.*[6]

During liminal seasons we find ourselves in the space between the familiar and the unfamiliar, and this can be challenging, disorienting, and unsettling. It is a season when we say goodbye to some of our old traditions and explore new ways of doing things. We encounter different liminal seasons in our lives all the time.

Some of these seasons can be challenging, and some of them can be quite exciting. Pregnancy is a liminal time when you await the arrival of a newborn child. Dropping your kid off at college as they leave the nest and start to gain independence is another liminal experience. Fall is also a liminal season when the leaves are changing, when it's no longer summer, and it's not yet winter.

However, oftentimes, these are the moments in life that help us define who we are. Life is full of interruptions and intrusions which lead us on new paths and take us to places we never imagined we would go. In these life interruptions, good and bad, is when we often see God doing God's greatest work.

I'm reminded of a song by my favorite band, Foo Fighters, entitled "Times Like These." This song took on a special meaning for me during the COVID-19 pandemic, as it did for many people. Even though the song was released several years ago, it was performed on the night of Joe Biden's Presidential Inauguration in 2021, and an episode of Saturday Night Live in 2020, because of its relevancy. It speaks to this idea of finding hope and truth in the midst of a liminal time. The chorus of the song says:

It's times like these you learn to live again.
It's times like these you give and give again.
It's times like these you learn to love again.
It's times like these time and time again.[7]

21

In liminal seasons we learn to live, and give, and love in new and profound ways. Liminal seasons offer opportunities to learn more about who we are and what is important to us. These times can offer us insight and allow us to gain a sense of perspective. We often see God working most clearly during these liminal times, and the story of Mary and Joseph is no exception.

Still, I'm sure Joseph must have had a difficult time processing his wife's pregnancy. This is especially true because, at the time, he thought that she had committed adultery. In the Gospel of Matthew (the only Gospel that includes the Annunciation to Joseph), we only get a snapshot of Joseph's response to Mary's pregnancy. In fact, Joseph never actually speaks a single word in the entire New Testament. On the other hand, when Mary finds out about her pregnancy, she sings an inspiring and uplifting song of praise called The Magnificat (which we will explore in the next chapter). Joseph, however, is quiet. We never hear from the actual mouth of Joseph.

Joseph's Decision

In the wake of first learning about Mary's pregnancy, we can only imagine the fear, anxiety, doubt, and sense of betrayal that Joseph must have felt. In his book *Faithful: Christmas Through the Eyes of Joseph*, Adam Hamilton writes:

> *The news that Joseph received from Mary was devastating... Joseph and Mary were not yet living together as husband and wife, but Joseph undoubtedly felt utterly betrayed and humiliated. Once Mary became visibly pregnant, people were going to talk.*[8]

Although Mary and Joseph were not officially married, their engagement, which followed typical Jewish marriage customs, acted almost like a contract. Scholars explain that Mary and Joseph's engagement was a binding arrangement which legally considered them to be husband and wife. Therefore, any unfaithfulness would be considered adultery, and their union could only be dissolved by death or divorce.[9]

Mary finds herself in an especially vulnerable state. According to the Law of Moses, the penalty for those caught in adultery is death. The Law states:

> *If there is a young woman, a virgin already engaged to be married, and a man meets her in the town and lies with her, you shall bring both of them to the gate of that town and stone them to death, the young woman because she did not cry for help in the town and the man because he violated his neighbor's wife. So, you shall purge the evil from your midst.*
>
> —Deuteronomy 22:23-24

Joseph could seek revenge against Mary if he wanted. He legally has every right to bring these charges against Mary. He has every right to invoke capital punishment against her by the Law of Moses. But Joseph decides to divorce Mary quietly instead. However, Joseph dismisses Mary with great risk to himself and his own reputation.

As Mary's child grows within her, people would begin to notice that she was pregnant and presume that Joseph was the father. Then, Joseph could be seen as dishonorable for abandoning his pregnant fiancé to carry and raise their child without him. In other words, Joseph would spare Mary's life, but he would take on all of the blame.

Out of compassion for Mary, Joseph, who is considered to be a righteous man, decides to essentially spare her. Joseph sees the importance of offering grace and love to Mary instead of punishment and death.

The Law of Love

This story reminds me of another story about Mary's own son. When Jesus is grown up, he follows in Joseph's footsteps and saves another woman from being stoned for alleged adultery. In John 8:1-11, the Pharisees bring a woman caught in adultery to Jesus and say, "The Law of Moses commands us to stone her, but what do you say?"

Jesus confronts the Pharisees and the crowds who are ready to condemn this woman by saying, "Let anyone among you who is without sin cast the first stone." When the Pharisees and the crowds hear this, they clear out until it is just Jesus and the woman. Then, Jesus asks the woman, "Where did everyone go? Has no one condemned you?" The woman responds, "No! No one has condemned me." To which Jesus replies, "Well, neither do I. Go and sin no more."

Just like Jesus, the child who will be born to Mary, Joseph decides to follow the call to show God's love, even though it violates the Law of Moses. Joseph practices a message that Jesus will preach and proclaim throughout his ministry. His righteousness is based on his ability to offer love and mercy over strictly following the law. Joseph practices what Mary's unborn child will later preach as an adult:

You shall love the Lord your God with all your heart, and with all your soul, and with all your mind. This is the greatest and first commandment. And a second is like it: You shall love your neighbor as yourself. On these two commandments hang all the law and the prophets.

—Matthew 22:37-40

Joseph understood the importance of showing love over following the letter of the law. This is something we see Jesus live out in his ministry time and time again. Jesus heals the sick and diseased on the sabbath. He touches the unclean. He challenges the cultural climate by eating with sinners and tax collectors. Jesus values human beings over the strict rules, laws, and customs that dictated much of Jewish society. Jesus offers grace and love over following the letter of the law. In his act of mercy for Mary, Joseph shows us the importance of grace. One might say that Joseph even acted as a forerunner for Jesus and his ministry.

Joseph's Dream

We can see that Joseph is indeed a righteous man. He is striving to do good in the midst of a bad situation but before Joseph could put his plan of quietly divorcing Mary into practice, he receives a strange dream. An angel of the Lord appears to Joseph in his dream saying:

Joseph, son of David, do not be afraid to take Mary as your wife, for the child conceived in her is from the Holy Spirit. She will bear a son, and you are to

25

name him Jesus, for he will save his people from their sins.

—Matthew 1:20, 21

Joseph is a dreamer, and he shares his name with another dreamer who is a character from the Old Testament. In the book of Genesis, we see that Joseph is sold into slavery in Egypt by his own brothers because of his dream that showed his brothers bowing down before him. His gift of interpreting dreams allows him to find favor with Pharaoh. Then, his dreams allow him to foresee a famine which allows Pharaoh to prepare and store up plenty of grain.

In the end, his initial dream comes true when his brothers travel to Egypt in search of food and bow down before their brother. Joseph's dreams take him on a grand journey that eventually brings about hope and prosperity.

In the Christmas story, I can imagine Joseph responding to this dream with fear and anxiety. There is no doubt that this dream will take him on a grand journey. I can also imagine this dream came with a sense of relief and maybe even hope. Joseph is finally clued into the true details surrounding Mary's pregnancy.

Yes, Mary is still pregnant. Yes, Joseph is still not the father. But now Joseph knows the truth. This pregnancy is not the result of adultery. Mary was not unfaithful to him. Instead, this pregnancy comes from the Holy Spirit as a way for God to enter into the world in a new way and to save God's people. It fulfills the words of the prophet Isaiah:

Look, the virgin shall conceive and bear a son, and they shall name him Emmanuel, which means, "God is with us."

—Matthew 1:23

God is sending a child named Jesus, as the Incarnation, God made flesh. God is coming to us, in the flesh, in the form of a baby to restore humanity, to save the people from their sins. The story of Christmas is a story that tells us that God is with us. Christmas reminds us that God has not left us alone. God is not up in the clouds, removed from creation. Instead, God interrupts our lives and comes into the world at the most unexpected times and in the most unexpected ways. Through the good and the bad, we are not alone. In his dream, Joseph received the best news of all. God is with us.

Emmanuel, God is with Us

John Wesley, the founder of the Methodist movement, lived a long and faithful life as a disciple of Jesus. He died in the year 1791 at the age of 87. Betsy Ritchie, John Wesley's housekeeper, wrote down a detailed account of John's final days on his deathbed, surrounded by his friends. She writes:

Finding we could not understand what he said, he paused a little, and then with all the remaining strength he had, cried out, "The best of all is, God is with us"; and then, as if to assert the faithfulness of our promise-keeping Jehovah and comfort the hearts of his weeping friends, lifting up his dying arm in token of victory and raising his feeble voice with a holy triumph not to be expressed, again re-

27

peated the heart-reviving, words, "The best of all is, God is with us!"[10]

"The best of all is, God is with us!" I wonder if this might also be a prayer that Joseph might have prayed himself. Joseph receives this news from the angel of the Lord telling him to take Mary as his wife because her child is the Messiah; and he is to name the child Jesus. Joseph is obedient to the angel's message:

Joseph awoke from sleep, he did as the angel of the Lord commanded him; he took her as his wife, but had no marital relations with her until she had borne a son; and he named him Jesus.
—Matthew 1:24, 25

Joseph wakes up and does exactly what the angel of the Lord tells him to do. He takes Mary as his wife, and when she gives birth to the child, he names him Jesus. In doing this, Joseph becomes the second disciple, after Mary, to receive the good news of Jesus Christ. In receiving this good news, Joseph essentially adopts Jesus into his own family. In fact, at the beginning of the Gospel of Matthew 1:1-17, we see a genealogy of Jesus' ancestry which ends saying:

Joseph the husband of Mary, of whom Jesus was born, who is called the Messiah.
—Matthew 1:1-17

Joseph's lineage connects Jesus through an ancestry of folks like Abraham, Solomon, and David who are pillars of the Jewish faith. This genealogy even includes some unlikely characters like Tamar, Rahab, and Ruth who are all non-Jewish women. Joseph brings Jesus along into a rich historical tradition. He welcomes him into the family and officially takes on the role of stepfather to the Messiah.

A few years ago, a small local theater where I live in Athens, Tennessee put on a wonderful production of the play *Shadowlands*. The play is based on the true story of C.S. Lewis who started corresponding with an American woman named Joy Davidman. Joy was a divorced mother with two boys named David and Douglas. Over time C.S. Lewis and Joy fell in love. In 1956 they were married, despite Joy's cancer diagnosis. In that same year, Lewis made the decision to adopt Joy's two sons.

Then, only four years later, C.S. Lewis finds himself as the sole caregiver of David and Douglas after Joy dies of cancer. Together, C.S. Lewis, David, and Douglas grieved the loss of Joy, but C.S. Lewis took his responsibility as stepfather very seriously. He treated his stepsons as if they were his own children. He loved them, provided for them, and cared for them throughout his life. Fifty years after his death, C.S. Lewis' stepson Douglas wrote a very personal reflection about his stepfather, whom he lovingly called "Jack," saying:

> *My first encounter with him was extra-ordinary. I was an 8-year-old American schoolboy, 'straight off the boat', brought to Oxford a short while after arriving in the strange land of England. I was being taken to meet the man who, as far as I was concerned, actually knew High King Peter of Narnia and the great lion Aslan. But in the kitchen of his house, 'The Kilns', we were greeted by a slightly stooped, balding, round-shouldered being with long nicotine-stained fingers and teeth, dressed in the shabbiest clothes I had ever seen. Despite my initial*

29

dismay, Jack soon emerged from my imaginary C.S. Lewis to become a real friend and a much-loved stepfather.[11]

We see Joseph in a similar role as the stepfather of Jesus. In the Gospels, we see Joseph care for Mary as she gives birth to Jesus in Bethlehem. We see Joseph move Mary and Jesus to Egypt as they live as refugees, fleeing the wrath of King Herod. We see Joseph bring his family out of Egypt and provide a home for them in the town of Nazareth. As Adam Hamilton writes:

The mission given to Joseph was to raise this boy as though he were Joseph's own. It was to love him, mentor him, teach him, and guide him. It was to model for this child what it meant to be a man – a man who honored and served God. Jesus was not Joseph's child by birth, but the boy would need Joseph to love him as his own.[12]

Joseph was put in a difficult situation. Would he believe the angel's message? Would he take Mary as his wife? Would he raise the child as his own? In the end, Joseph held on to the hope that he found in the promise of Jesus, Emmanuel. In the end, Joseph could proclaim that God was with him. We too have the opportunity to accept this message of hope into our own lives.

God of hope and peace, we thank you for the example of Joseph who responded to your call with obedience and faithfulness. Help us to find ways to live into that same example and to experience the gift of Christ who dwells among us, in the flesh. We thank you for the ways that you work in our lives, even when you work

through what might seem like unwelcome interrup-
tions. May you continue to work on our hearts as we
prepare for the coming of your Son at Christmas. We
thank you for the continued hope that we find in the
uncertainty of life. Amen.

Reflection Questions

1. Joseph essentially became Jesus' stepfather. Can you think of someone in your own life (grandparents, aunts, uncles, cousins, close friends) whom you looked up to and acted as another parental figure?

2. The news of an unexpected pregnancy was a shock for Mary and Joseph. Can you think of a time in your own life when you were thrown for a loop and were faced with something unexpected?

3. Joseph learns that his fiancé Mary is pregnant, and he knows that he is not the father. In hearing this news, we can imagine the pain, disappointment, and sense of betrayal that Joseph must have felt. Even if it is not as severe as Joseph's situation, have you ever experienced a situation when someone you trusted let you down? How did you handle your feelings of pain and disappointment?

4. According to the Law of Moses, the penalty for those caught in adultery is death. Joseph legally had every right to bring these charges against Mary, but he decides to offer grace by dismissing her quietly. Can you think of a time in your own life when someone offered you grace instead of punishment? How did that experience impact your life?

5. The angel of the Lord appears to Joseph in a dream telling him that Mary's pregnancy comes from the Holy Spirit. Joseph is told to take Mary as his wife, and her child will be Emmanuel, God with us. How have you experienced God's presence with you in your own life?

CHAPTER THREE

MARY
HOPE FOR JUSTICE

Hannah prayed and said,
"My heart exults in the Lord;
my strength is exalted in my God.
My mouth derides my enemies,
because I rejoice in my victory."
—2 Samuel 2:1

And Mary said,
"My soul magnifies the Lord,
and my spirit rejoices in God my Savior,
for he has looked with favor on the lowliness of his
servant. Surely, from now on all generations will
call me blessed; for the Mighty One has done great
things for me, and holy is his name.
His mercy is for those who fear him
from generation to generation."
—Luke 1:46-50

My wife Ally has a beautiful singing voice, and I am always requesting her to sing songs for Sunday morning worship. Every Christmas, I ask her to sing one of my favorite Christmas songs. The song, originally performed by Francesca Battistelli and written by Nichole Nordeman, is called "Be Born in Me." It is a beautiful song that speaks from the perspective of Mary as she grapples with the news of her unexpected pregnancy. The song goes like this:

Everything inside me wants to hide
Is this shadow, an angel or a warrior?
If God is pleased with me, why am I so terrified?

Someone tell me I am only dreaming
Somehow help me see with Heaven's eyes
And before my head agrees, my heart is on its knees

Holy is He, blessed am I

Be born in me, be born in me
Trembling heart, somehow, I believe
That You chose me

I'll hold you in the beginning
You will hold me in the end
Every moment in the middle
Make my heart your Bethlehem
Be born in me.[13]

In this chapter, we will explore the hope for justice that Mary expresses in her song. Mary's song, which is known as The Magnificat, gives us a glimpse into how Mary must have felt when, out of the blue, an angel appears to her and brings about this news of disruption into her life. This unexpected news surely brought forth feelings of anxiety, fear, and confusion. The angel tells Mary:

> *Do not be afraid, Mary, for you have found favor with God. And now, you will conceive in your womb and bear a son, and you will name him Jesus. He will be great, and will be called the Son of the Most High, and the Lord God will give to him the throne of his ancestor David. He will reign over the house of Jacob forever, and of his kingdom there will be no end.*
>
> —Luke 1:30-33

The angel tells her to not be afraid, because she is highly favored by God. In fact, she is so lucky that, even though she is a virgin, she will bear a son who will be the Messiah. Now, if this is what it means to be highly favored by God, then I don't think I want to be!

Mary is a young girl. She is engaged to be married to her fiancé Joseph. In the last chapter we talked about how the news of a pregnancy could ruin everything and even opens her up to the possibility of being accused of adultery and stoned to death. This news radically changes the trajectory of her life, but, in the midst of this unexpected news, Mary responds with courage, obedience, and faith.

Mary is often portrayed as a young, fearful, and naïve teenager, but the Gospel of Luke paints a very different picture of Mary. After learning about her miraculous pregnancy, Mary is told by the angel that her relative, Elizabeth, is also pregnant. This prompts Mary to journey nine long and difficult days in order to visit Elizabeth. She travels seventy miles from Jerusalem to the Judean town in the hill country with no Joseph by her side. As far as we know, she does this completely this alone. She travels in order to visit her older relatives Elizabeth and Zechariah. This shows that Mary is resilient, strong, and motivated. Mary is up to the task.

Elizabeth and Zechariah

Interestingly enough, Elizabeth and Zechariah are dealing with news of their own unexpected pregnancy. After years and years of hoping for a child, Elizabeth and her husband Zechariah had given up. Imagine the sense of sorrow and pain they must have experienced during this time. This was before in vitro fertilization. I know there are a lot of folks who experience this sense of loss and pain as well. So, we can see how painful this must have been for Elizabeth and Zechariah. They desperately wanted a child. In their old age, they had faced the fact that they would never have kids, or so they thought.

It all changed one day while Zechariah was serving as a priest in the Temple. He was in the Holy of Holies which was the most sacred room in the Temple. This was the place where the people believed that God's presence was most made known. And while Zechariah was in this room, an angel appears to him and says:

Do not be afraid, Zechariah, for your prayer has been heard. Your wife Elizabeth will bear you a son, and you will name him John. You will have joy and gladness, and many will rejoice at his birth, for he will be great in the sight of the Lord. He must never drink wine or strong drink; even before his birth he will be filled with the Holy Spirit. He will turn many of the people of Israel to the Lord their God. With

the spirit and power of Elijah he will go before him, to turn the hearts of parents to their children, and the disobedient to the wisdom of the righteous, to make ready a people prepared for the Lord.
—Luke 1:13-17

Zechariah hears about this unexpected pregnancy of a child who will be known as John the Baptist. And, at first, Zechariah does not believe the angel. He responds to the angel saying:

How will I know that this is so?
For I am an old man, and my wife is getting on in years.
—Luke 1:18

Zechariah acknowledges his old age, but I want you to notice that he does not call his wife old. He just politely adds that his wife "is getting on in years." Zechariah is full of doubt. This news seems inconceivable; however, this story sounds a lot like another story in the Old Testament. Abraham and Sarah had also longed for a child, and in their old age they are told that they are going to have a baby – and they name their son Isaac who becomes one of the fathers of the Hebrew people. Likewise, Zechariah is told of a son – who he is to name John – who will play a vital role in the history of humanity. And, understandably, Zechariah has a hard time believing this.

But the Angel Gabriel, who does not seem as understanding, responds to Zechariah's doubt by saying:

But now, because you did not believe my words, which will be fulfilled in their time, you will become mute, unable to speak, until the day these things oc-cur.

—Luke 1:20

When Zechariah leaves the Temple, he isn't able to speak. Just as the Angel Gabriel said, Zechariah is silent throughout Elizabeth's pregnancy. When Elizabeth discovers that she is pregnant, she goes into seclusion for several months during her pregnancy. Elizabeth and Zechariah have completely closed themselves off from their neighbors, their friends, and their family. They are in seclusion.

I'm sure they were full of questions such as: How are we going to have this baby at such an old age? How are we going to have the energy to raise a child? Why now? Why after all these years would God give us a baby now? It seems, however, that the joy of a promised child overshadowed all of their doubts. Elizabeth demonstrates great faith and rejoices in her miraculous pregnancy.

Mary and Elizabeth's Kinship

Mary and Elizabeth are confronting very similar circumstances. Both of them are dealing with unusual pregnancies. Elizabeth is in the midst of a post-menopausal, geriatric pregnancy; while Mary, a virgin, is pregnant from the Holy Spirit. They are both surprised by the child that they carry in their womb. Both of these pregnancies should be completely impossible. And this is what makes Elizabeth the perfect person for Mary to visit and confide in. Elizabeth is dealing with a similar miraculous situation.

Mary enters the house of Zechariah and greets Elizabeth. When Elizabeth hears Mary's greeting, Elizabeth's child leaps in her womb and she is filled with the Holy Spirit. Her child, whom we know as John the Baptist, proclaims about the hope of Christ even from his mother's belly. Elizabeth, who is filled with hope, blesses Mary saying:

Blessed are you among women, and blessed is the fruit of your womb. And why has this happened to me; that the mother of my Lord come to me? For as soon as I heard the sound of your greeting, the child in my womb leaped for joy.

And blessed is she who believed that there would be a fulfillment of what was spoken to her by the Lord.
—Luke 1:42, 43

From the very moment Mary walked into the door, Elizabeth knew and recognized that the child in Mary's womb was the Son of God. She proclaimed Jesus as "my Lord" before he was even born. This moment must have given Mary the affirmation that she was needing. Elizabeth is essentially corroborating the angel's story. Elizabeth is telling Mary that she truly is carrying the Son of the Most-High God. The angel was, in fact, telling the truth.

I can just imagine Mary's sigh of relief when she hears Elizabeth's words. Mary had been hiding this secret and was uncertain, afraid, and anxious. But before she has a chance to try to explain to Elizabeth what has happened, Elizabeth shows Mary that she already knows her secret. And Elizabeth is actually filled with joy on Mary's behalf. Her beloved relative believes this miraculous story of a virgin conception. She believes this totally unbelievable story.

The Magnificat

Mary cannot contain herself. She is so filled with hope that she sings a song known as The Magnificat, which in Latin means "magnifies." The Magnificat is a psalm of praise that bursts forth from her heart and comes from the Holy Spirit.

This song is closely paralleled to the prayer of Hannah. In First Samuel, Hannah's prayer begins, *My heart exults in the Lord; my strength is exalted in my God.* Likewise, Mary begins her song by singing, *My soul magnifies the Lord, and my spirit rejoices in God my Savior.* Both Mary and Hannah sing about God's ability to bring about justice and hope. Hannah sings:

> *The Lord makes poor and makes rich; he brings low, he also exalts.*
> *He raises up the poor from the dust; he lifts the needy from the ash heap, to make them sit with prince sand inherit a seat of honor.*
> *For the pillars of the earth are the Lord's, and on them he has set the world.*
>
> —1 Samuel 2:7, 8

Like Hannah, Mary sings as if all the injustices of the world have already been made right. She sings:

> *His mercy is for those who fear him from generation to generation. He has shown strength with his arm; he has scattered the proud in the thoughts of their hearts. He has brought down the powerful from their thrones, and lifted up the lowly; he has filled*

the hungry with good things, and sent the rich away
empty.

—Luke 1:50-53

Mary is speaking as a prophet, singing a song about a God who comes down as in human form to bring about radical transformation. Mary, a young vulnerable girl who knows the effects of poverty has been chosen. She is humble, she is poor, and she is vulnerable, but God speaks through Mary anyway. She is a young woman who lives in a depressed region of Judea. Her words are about how God redefines the way the world works. She sings about a God who is interested in reversing the roles of the rich and the poor. God uses a poor girl to speak about the injustice of poverty. The Protestant Reformer, Martin Luther, says:

> *[The Magnificat] constrains you to fear if you are*
> *mighty, and to take comfort if you are of low de-*
> *gree. And the mightier you are, the more must you*
> *fear; the lowlier you are, the more must you take*
> *comfort.*[14]

God tends to align with the marginalized, the poor, and the oppressed. We see examples of this throughout the history of the Hebrew people. Out of a burning bush, God calls Moses to deliver God's people out of slavery, saying:

> *I have observed the misery of my people who are in*
> *Egypt; I have heard their cry on account of their*
> *taskmasters. Indeed, I know their sufferings, and I*
> *have come down to deliver them from the Egyp-*
> *tians, and to bring them up out of that land to a*
> *good and broad land, a land flowing with milk and*

honey, to the country of the Canaanites, the Hittites, the Amorites, the Perizzites, the Hivites, and the Jebusites. The cry of the Israelites has now come to me; I have also seen how the Egyptians oppress them.

So come, I will send you to Pharaoh to bring my people, the Israelites, out of Egypt.

—Exodus 3:7-10

Throughout the New Testament, we also see Jesus aligning himself with the marginalized, the poor, and the oppressed. Jesus consistently spends time with the sinners and tax collectors. He often spends time with the marginalized and the outcast. This behavior gets him in a lot of trouble with the Pharisees and all the religious people, because Jesus is constantly breaking down the barriers that hold certain people back. Jesus is constantly tearing down the walls that exclude the outsiders. He is quick to call out the insiders and rebuke the rich. Jesus has come to right the wrongs in our society, to bring about justice, and to bring hope to the hopeless.

Call for Justice

In her pregnancy, Mary proclaims Jesus' message, even as Jesus sits in her womb. She tells us that God has scattered the proud, brought down the powerful, and sent the rich away. Instead of lifting up the powerful, God has lifted up the lowly, filled the hungry, and helped the servant.

Mary sings about a God who levels the playing field when it comes to the socioeconomic arena. She is, in fact, prophesying about the very things that her son will do. She claims that God's name is magnified when justice prevails and the lowly and marginalized are lifted up. God is magnified when the rich are brought low and the poor are raised up. Mary sings a song of hope for justice in an unjust world. As Bishop Will Willimon writes:

> *To us, this looks like a world turned upside down, but Mary has the eyes of faith to see that this great reversal is actually the power of God to turn the world right side up.*[15]

This passage teaches us that God cares deeply about people. God cares deeply about the people who go hungry and go without. God cares deeply about injustice, suffering, and inequality. God cares deeply about the people who are often ignored. God is here and God is involved because God cares. This passage teaches us that God doesn't just favor the rich, but God also cares for the poor.

How fitting that Mary, a humble servant of God, would give birth to Jesus who has come to serve. As the Gospel of Mark says:

> *For the Son of Man came not to be served but to serve, and to give his life a ransom for many.*
> —Mark 10:45

Jesus exemplifies what it means to be a servant. It was Jesus who reached out to the prostitutes and tax collectors. It was Jesus who welcomed the stranger and the outcast. It was Jesus who took a washcloth and basin and washed the feet of the disciples. It was Jesus who went to the cross and sacrificed himself even though we didn't deserve it. This is the God that Mary is singing about.

Jesus lived out his ministry reaching out to the least and the lost. In the New Testament, Jesus continually favors the lowly, the economically deprived, the vulnerable, the oppressed, the broken, and the marginalized. This is the God that Mary is singing about.

Mary has experienced radical transformation. God has transformed her life the way that pregnancy has transformed her body. God's divinity has transformed her humanity. By singing this song, Mary is calling on us to be agents of change as well. Mary's song is an invitation for us to seek paths of social justice in our communities and around the world.

There is a great need for justice in our world today, and we are called to bring about justice in places of injustice. According to a 2019 study by the United Nations, we produce enough food to feed everyone on the planet. We can literally feed everyone in the world. However, hunger is still prevalent in many parts of the world. In fact, around 821 million people are chronically undernourished.[16]

My supermarket is just a few miles from my home, and I am never in a position where I do not have access to fresh food. My pantry and refrigerator are always full. There are hundreds of restaurants at my immediate disposal. And yet, there are millions of people who are starving. Hunger and poverty are the kinds of injustices that Mary cries out against in her Magnificat. We have a responsibility to play a role in bringing hope to the hopeless.

In the midst of the coronavirus pandemic in 2020, an article came out from the Holston Conference newsletter, *The Call*, about a grant from our Holston Annual Conference. This grant went to provide more than 2,500 people in East Africa new cloth masks, hand sanitizer, and gloves so that they can protect themselves from getting or spreading COVID-19. They receive the basic essentials which we really have been taking for granted. I had no problem getting cloth masks or hand sanitizer and, before I saw this article, it never occurred to me that there were people out there to whom these necessary products were not available.

The mission supervisor for the United Methodist Church in South Sudan, Jaka Joice, proposed this project back in October. And by mid-November, they had distributed 2,584 masks, 34 large bottles of sanitizer, and 17 boxes of gloves to congregations in Uganda, South Sudan, and Congo. Joice wrote about the distribution, saying:

> *People were very happy to receive the masks, and they arrived very timely when [the coronavirus] is spreading very rapidly in Uganda with many rampant deaths.*[17]

This is the kind of work that Mary is calling us to do in her song. We are called to play a part in setting things right. We are called to partner with God in God's plan for this world. We are called to reach out to the lonely, lost, and hurting of this world. We are called to make a difference in the lives of others in the name of Jesus Christ.

This pregnancy didn't just change the trajectory of Mary's life, but it has changed the trajectory of our lives as well. We are called to do God's work as we strive to bring about hope for justice, change, and transformation. Mary is crying out to us. She is inviting us to be a part of her son's mission. We are invited to look around at the examples of injustice and oppression in our own neighborhoods. We are called to find ways to right wrongs and reach out to the oppressed. We are called to speak up for those who cannot speak for themselves. We are called to make a difference for Jesus.

God of hope, peace, joy, and love we join along with Mary as we celebrate the hope for justice expressed in her song. We long for the day when we might see the poor and lowly raised up. We know there is so much pain and injustice in our world, but we cling to the hope in the promise of your son, the Messiah. May we find ways to bring about hope and justice in the lives of those around us. May you continue to work on our hearts as we strive to do your work in the world. Amen.

Reflection Questions

1. The Magnificat, is considered to be one of the very first Christmas carols. What is your favorite Christmas carol or Christmas song? What is it about that song that speaks to you?

2. Mary goes to visit her relative Elizabeth (who is pregnant with John the Baptist) after she hears the angel's news that she would bear the Son of God. Who would you most want to talk to or be with upon hearing strange or disturbing or exciting news like that?

3. Mary sings a song praising God's great reversal. God lifts up the lowly, the poor and powerless, and brings down the high and mighty, the powerful and proud. Have you ever experienced a reversal of fortune in your own life? How does Mary's song speak to you personally in your own life?

4. In Mary's song of praise, she echoes Hannah, the mother of the first prophet Samuel in the Old Testament. Hannah sings praises to a God who reverses the fortune of others. Where do you witness this longing for a reversal of fortunes in our own day?

5. What are some of the injustices that you have witnessed in your communities and neighborhoods? What are some ways that you can join Jesus' mission to bring hope to the hopeless?

CHAPTER FOUR

SHEPHERDS
HOPE PROCLAIMED

The people who walked in darkness have seen a great light; those who lived in a land of deep darkness—on them light has shined... For a child has been born for us, a son given to us; authority rests upon his shoulders; and he is named Wonderful Counselor, Mighty God, Everlasting Father, Prince of Peace.
                                                    —Isaiah 9:2,6

In that region there were shepherds living in the fields, keeping watch over their flock by night. Then an angel of the Lord stood before them, and the glory of the Lord shone around them, and they were terrified. But the angel said to them, "Do not be afraid; for see—I am bringing you good news of great joy for all the people: to you is born this day in the city of David a Savior, who is the Messiah, the Lord. This

49

will be a sign for you: you will find a child wrapped in bands of cloth and lying in a manger."

—Luke 2:8-12

One of my favorite bands is Steve Martin and the Steep Canyon Rangers. It combines two of my favorite things – banjos and Steve Martin. And on their last album, they came out with a song called "The Strangest Christmas Yet." Throughout the song, Steve Martin sings about he and his wife inviting family, in-laws, and third cousins to their home for Christmas. Grandma brings a pumpkin pie that tastes like her cigar. Uncle Don parks in the front yard. All the kids start a fire in the driveway. Cousin Billy is watching out for invaders from the planet Zarn.

All these crazy and strange things happen as the family gathers for Christmas. Maybe some of y'all can see some similarities in your own family gatherings. But the song ends saying: "It's the strangest Christmas yet. It'll take some time to forget the strangest Christmas yet."[18]

The First Christmas

I couldn't help but think that the original Christmas story is pretty strange. It is not as flowery and perfect as we sometimes like to think it is. Here we have this poor, young couple, Mary and Joseph, who are told by the Angel Gabriel that – even though Mary is a virgin – she will give birth to the Son of God. After an angel visits Joseph in a dream, Joseph makes the decision to stick with Mary and believe that God is working in this situation. Then, as Mary's pregnancy progresses to her final trimester, they are forced to travel from their home in Nazareth all the way to the town of Bethlehem.

Their home of Israel is occupied by the Roman Government, and the Emperor Caesar Augustus issues a decree that says everyone must go to their hometown in order to be registered. And this probably has more to do with taxes than anything else. The Roman Government was known for imposing harsh taxes on the people.

Mary and Joseph make this 90-mile journey that takes them across some difficult terrain. They go south along the flatlands of the Jordan River, then west over the hills surrounding Jerusalem, and finally on into Bethlehem. It is a grueling trip – especially for Mary who is about to give birth to the Son of God.

Once they arrive in the town of Bethlehem, things just seem to get even worse, because the time comes for Mary to give birth to her baby. Unfortunately, there is no place for them in the local inn. They are forced to give birth in a less than ideal place. There is no Holiday Inn Express to take reservations. There is no hospital that can help deliver the child in a safe and sterile environment. Mary cannot even give birth in the comfort of her own home with no queen bed, no tub, no pillows, or blankets. Instead, Mary gives birth and wraps her child in strips of cloth and places him in a manger.

This just seems like a cruel joke. Mary and Joseph just cannot seem to catch a break. Their child, the Son of God, is brought into this world through very humble beginnings, and this trend continues on. Even as an adult, Jesus never really lived a life of comfort and luxury. In fact, it seems fitting that Jesus was placed in a manger instead of a crib because, at one point, Jesus even said:

> *Foxes have holes, and birds of the air have nests; but the Son of Man has nowhere to lay his head.*
> —Matthew 8:20

Jesus is born in a very humble, barn-like, atmosphere. Jesus was born into poverty. It's ironic that the celebration of this birth has turned into a commercialized spectacle.

Commercialized Christmas

I recently went up to the mall in Knoxville, and I was trying to find the last few Christmas gifts I needed to buy. The traffic was horrible. I couldn't get over in the lane I needed to, so I had to turn back around and try again. Then as I made my way into the parking lot, I passed some police surveillance cameras. And next to the cameras was a sign that said, "Lock your car doors and hide your gifts." I parked in the last parking spot furthest from the door, in a long row full of cars. I finally entered the mall and went inside a few shops, trying to find those perfect Christmas gifts for my friends and family.

After a few moments, I found one gift that I really liked. It was a modest Nativity scene carved out of wood. It was in one piece and pretty small; it just had Mary, Joseph, and baby Jesus under a little roof. I thought to myself, "Oh, this would be a perfect gift to give my parents." Maybe this whole shopping experience won't be as painful as I thought. Then I looked at the price tag. $148.00. This led me to think, "I wonder what Jesus might say about all this?"

Jesus' birth has turned into an excuse for us to feed our need for consumerism. Sure, we buy gifts for others, but we expect gifts in return. We feel as if we have to take advantage of all the holiday sales. Each year we purchase more and more as we play into this commercialized season.

Now, I don't want to come across as too cynical. But I just think that we can sometimes go overboard. We sometimes miss the point. It just seems ironic that a store would charge $148.00 for a small piece of wood depicting a scene of the birth of Jesus Christ – one who was born in a barn and placed in a manger.

The Old Testament prophet Isaiah tells us something very different. In Isaiah 9:6 we are told of a child that has been born for us, a son given. We weren't charged $148.00. This wasn't a special holiday sale that was offered to us. Isaiah says that unto us the greatest gift has been given for free.

The Prophet Isaiah

Isaiah prophesied about this birth long ago and talks about the contrast between darkness and light. He speaks of those who have walked in darkness who finally see a great light. This darkness represents a difficult period in the nation of Israel. Isaiah writes during the Syro-Ephraimite war. During this time King Ahaz is dealing with conflict between Assyria and an anti-Assyrian coalition. King Ahaz is unsure of what to do.

There is panic. The people don't feel safe. The people have experienced war, violence, and oppression. They distrust the government and the leadership. Isaiah speaks in this dark time, when folks look at their lives and can't see any hope of a future. It is almost as if they are walking blindly, not knowing what is ahead of them.

Perhaps the darkness also represents our own circumstances. We live in a world where there is death, destruction, and disease. We are navigating a global pandemic with the coronavirus. We lose loved ones to cancer and sickness or even through cruel circumstances and accidents. As we reflect, we can remember all the shootings and acts of violence that our world has experienced. At times, it can feel like we are walking blindly, not knowing what is ahead of us. In this dark context, Isaiah writes this poem; he writes this song of good news letting us know that we won't be left in the dark. He says:

The people who walked in darkness have seen a great light; those who lived in a land of deep darkness— on them light has shined.

—Isaiah 9:2

Scholars believe that this song was originally part of a coronation service for a Judean King. This song was *not* originally composed with Jesus in mind. Instead, most scholars believe that it was specifically written for King Ahaz's son, King Hezekiah. Hezekiah was the thirteenth king of Judah, and he was considered to be very righteous according to the book of Kings. He was a huge improvement from the kings who had preceded him. Hezekiah was a good ruler. He enacted religious reforms and created a strict

54

mandate for the sole worship of the God of Israel. He also prohibited any worship of false idols.

Isaiah sings a song which seems to be a political promise more than anything else. Isaiah speaks of a baby who will be a political figure of authority – a baby who will bring peace, security, and justice to Israel. That's a lot of pressure to put on an infant. But Israel is threatened to be annihilated by the Assyrians at any moment. And Isaiah says:

For a child has been born for us, a son given to us; authority rests upon his shoulders; and he is named Wonderful Counselor, Mighty God, Everlasting Father, Prince of Peace.

—Isaiah 9:6

It seems strange, but this baby represents new life. This baby represents a fresh start. This baby represents hope. I don't know about you, but when I hear "For unto us a child is born. Unto us a son is given" Handel's *Messiah* comes to my mind. Isaiah offers words that make us think about the Christmas story. In fact, Isaiah is sometimes referred to as the "Christmas Prophet," because there seems to be a link between Isaiah and the Christmas story. Perhaps Isaiah is speaking about Jesus without even realizing it?

Christmas is always a special time because, despite all the shopping and chaos, it really is a season where we receive a special gift. Isaiah speaks of this gift that was given to us.

A Gift Given to Us

In 2018, there was a great commercial called "The Boy and the Piano." The commercial retraces key moments in Sir Elton John's career. We see Sir Elton playing in stadiums, traveling on a private jet, playing in a pub, and performing at school. The commercial ends with a 4-year-old Elton on Christmas morning. He eagerly runs down the stairs and receives the gift of a piano from his grandmother. This is undoubtedly the gift that would change his life forever. The commercial ends with a 71-year-old Elton sitting at that same piano. And these words flash across the screen: "Some gifts are more than just a gift."[19]

On Christmas morning we celebrate the gift of a newborn child, one who will be called: Wonderful Counselor, Mighty God, Everlasting Father, and Prince of Peace. Yes, this poem written by Isaiah was intended to be a royal coronation hymn and birth announcement of a new prince; but Isaiah seems to also broaden this message to a greater king who will one day come.

This song tells us that his government and his peace will have no end. It is a song of comfort in the midst of darkness. It is a song written for a baby who will change the way things have always been. It is the promise of a child of hope, a child of Bethlehem. It is a gift that has changed our lives.

The Shepherds

Surprisingly, on this night in Bethlehem, the gift of Christ is first presented to the shepherds who are out in the fields, watching their flock at night. And they are visited by an angel of the Lord who tells them:

Do not be afraid; for see I am bringing you good news of great joy for all the people: to you is born this day in the city of David a Savior, who is the Messiah, the Lord. This will be a sign for you: you will find a child wrapped in bands of cloth and lying in a manger.

—Luke 2:10-12

It is interesting that this message is first brought to these smelly, poor, humble shepherds. They are at the bottom of the socioeconomic ladder. They were poor and uneducated. They probably smelled. Many of them may have even been homeless. And yet, these are the first visitors to look upon the Christ Child. And it is not like there weren't other people in Bethlehem –because there was no room in the inn. It is a busy city with a lot of people, but these shepherds are the first ones to be invited to see the Son of God for themselves.

I think it is important to remember that Mary and Joseph are giving birth to this child in the little town of Bethlehem, the city of David. In the Old Testament, we are told of a young shepherd boy named David who became king of Israel. David described his important and dangerous work as a shepherd to his predecessor, Saul saying:

Your servant used to keep sheep for his father; and whenever a lion or a bear came, and took a lamb from the flock, I went after it and struck it down, rescuing the lamb from its mouth; and if it turned against me, I would catch it by the jaw, strike it

> *down, and kill it. Your servant has killed both lions and bears; and this uncircumcised Philistine shall be like one of them, since he has defied the armies of the living God.*
>
> —1 Samuel 17:34-36

Shepherds in ancient Israel had a very important job. This job was not for the faint of heart. It was a job that required 24/7 attention and devotion. Shepherds kept watch, kept the sheep fed, and kept dangerous animals away. They were tasked with protecting their flock of sheep.

Shepherds were sometimes forced to fight viciously against predatory animals, and even human predators, in order to defend their flock. They also searched for good pastures, searched for the lost sheep, and searched for the injured in their flock. They were also held accountable for the nourishment of their sheep, kept account of their numbers, and were answerable to their resources. It takes a lot of work to be a good shepherd.

But it is interesting to know that during the time of David, the title "shepherd" also had a royal connotation. Gods and kings were called the shepherd of their people. This is why I don't think it was a coincidence that these shepherds were among the first to witness the Christ Child.

In response to this angel's message, they immediately leave their sheep and run to greet this child. No one even stopped to ask, "Hey, what about the sheep? Do we need to go in shifts? Do we need to take turns?" Instead, they are convinced that something special has happened and they are invited to witness it. So, they all go to visit this baby in the manger.

And it is no wonder that they are convinced because, after they received this initial message from one angel, suddenly, there is a whole multitude of angels standing there and singing praises to God:

Glory to God in the highest heaven, and on earth peace among those whom he favors!
—Luke 2:14

It is remarkable that this multitude of angels would appear to none other than these shepherds. In his book *The Journey*, Adam Hamilton describes this encounter with the shepherds by saying:

Because most shepherds did not own their own land, they grazed their flocks on the land of their neighbors. Sometimes this created tension. Shepherds were tolerated but not always esteemed by their neighbors. When Luke tells us that shepherds were the first to be invited to see the Christ Child, first-century hearers would not have found this endearing, but shocking![20]

The message that we receive at Christmas is that Jesus came for all of us. And maybe that requires us to be vulnerable. All throughout Jesus' ministry, we see Jesus aligning himself more with the humble, the lowly, the sinners, and the marginalized. Jesus eats and drinks with sinners and tax collectors. And in those instances, we can see that Jesus has come for all people. Jesus has come for the preachers, teachers, lawyers, doctors, and even the shepherds. He has come for the vulnerable, and we are all vulnerable. Jesus has come for us.

We see the shepherds in this story, and it is easy to overlook them. But we can't do that. God has brought them to the forefront of the story. These shepherds, who have devoted their lives to caring for their sheep, can teach us some important lessons in our own lives.

Who are the shepherds in our own time? Who are the folks who are working diligently but who are often overlooked? Who are the people caring for the needs of others and ignoring their own needs?

I cannot help but think about our nurses, doctors, and health care workers who often work long and tireless shifts in order to help heal others. I cannot help but think about our janitors and custodians who clean and sanitize hospitals, schools, and churches so that people have clean spaces to live and work. I cannot help but think about our public-school teachers who work every day with very little pay or appreciation so that our children can be educated.

These are just some of the shepherds. The truth is, we are all called to be shepherds, to reach out to the vulnerable and care for the sick. We are all called to share hope with those who need it.

At Christmas, we celebrate the God who enters into our lives and comes among us in the flesh. We celebrate the love of God through the person of Jesus Christ. We celebrate the God who walks with us – even in the midst of our brokenness and sin. God has entered into this place with us. God has come to bring the light of Christ into the world.

Silent Night

I'm reminded of a story that took place on a very special Christmas Eve in the little Church of St. Nicholas. In this small church, in a village in Austria, the song *Silent Night* was first heard. A few days before Christmas, Josef Mohr walked to the home of Franz Gruber, the choir director and organist of the church. Mohr brought with him the words to a poem that he had written two years earlier. He asked Franz Gruber to compose a melody with the guitar. Legend has it that the aging church organ was broken and was in disrepair.[21]

That night in 1818, in St. Nicholas Church, the world heard in German for the first time "Silent Night." We still sing this simple, but very noble song many years later. This song captures the spirit of this night:

> *Silent night, holy night*
> *All is calm, all is bright*
> *Round yon Virgin, Mother and Child*
> *Holy Infant so tender and mild*
> *Sleep in heavenly peace*
> *Sleep in heavenly peace.*[22]

Now, for Mary and the newborn infant Jesus, I'm not sure how silent it really was. I'm sure the baby Jesus was crying and whining a little bit. But I think this story still captures the essence of one who would grow up and bring about peace in the midst of chaos. Two hundred years later we are still singing this song.

In fact, "Silent Night" is one of the most well-known songs in the world. It is a song that played a big role in 1914 during World War I. The fighting had only just begun on the Western Front but hope for a quick war was already gone. Both armies knew that this war would not have an easy resolution.

A system of trenches separated the two sides, with an area in-between them known as "No Man's Land." But on Christmas Eve, an unofficial truce began. German soldiers began singing "Silent Night" in German. After a few moments, soldiers on the opposing side began singing along in English. Soldiers –who hours before had been shooting at one another – were now singing together about the wonder of Christ's birth.

As the night and the singing continued, the soldiers emerged out of their trenches to join one another in "No Man's Land." An estimated 100,000 soldiers along the Western Front laid down their weapons that night and the next day. In the following years of the war, their commanders would demand that they continue fighting on Christmas Day.[23]

But on this one night in 1914, soldiers paused their fighting. For this one night there were no sounds of war – no shooting, no death. It really was a Silent Night. And for a brief moment, there really was peace on earth and goodwill toward men. For unto us a child is born. Unto us a son is given. In this promise, we find hope, knowing that God is with us.

O God, we celebrate the birth of your Son who has come into our world to live among us. We celebrate the Emmanuel, God with us. Thank you for letting your presence be known to us. May you remind us of your love and grace which is with us forever and always. As we think on this story of your birth, may you invite us, just as you did the shepherds, to come and share in your presence. Amen.

Reflection Questions

1. Have you ever received a gift that was more than just a gift? Have you ever received a gift that helped shape you into the person you are today?

2. Christmas is a special time when we experience the love of God that came down at Christmas. How have you experienced the love of Christ through the story of Christmas?

3. How might you find ways to share the love of God that came down at Christmas to the people in your own life?

4. The angels appeared to the lowly shepherds with the news of Jesus' birth. Who are those people in our society who would be like the shepherds? Who are the people that we look down on and keep at an arm's length? Who are the people that we try to avoid?

5. How might we find ways to shepherd others? How might we reach out to the vulnerable and care for the sick? How might we find ways to serve those around us who are in need?

CHAPTER FIVE

THE WISEMEN
HOPE PROCLAIMED

A multitude of camels shall cover you, the young camels of Midian and Ephah; all those from Sheba shall come. They shall bring gold and frankincense, and shall proclaim the praise of the Lord.
                                        —Isaiah 60:6

When they saw that the star had stopped, they were overwhelmed with joy. On entering the house, they saw the child with Mary his mother; and they knelt down and paid him homage. Then, opening their treasure chests, they offered him gifts of gold, frankincense, and myrrh. And having been warned in a dream not to return to Herod, they left for their own country by another road.
                                        —Matthew 2:10-12

One of my favorite movies growing up was a Disney classic called, *The Lion King*. This movie portrays the struggle between good and evil through the adventures of a lion cub named Simba. Simba is the son of the lion king, and he faces several challenges as he comes to terms with his royal heritage.

In the opening scene, the long-awaited announcement of Simba's birth is carried throughout Africa. Tribal drums and African chants are shouted during the cub's arrival. Elephants, gazelles, antelopes, vultures, zebras, and giraffes all journey to witness this young cub. They climb hills, descend sloping canyons, forge streams, and hike jungle paths. I imagine that some of them embarked upon long journeys in order to reach their destination.

Once all the animals arrive in adoration and praise, the infant cub is presented to them. Rafiki, a baboon, lifts the newborn high above his head to symbolize Simba's exalted calling. And the animals shout and praise this young cub.[24] This movie is a symbolic picture of the Son of God, who came into the world as an infant and was exalted as king.

The Lion King reminds me of the mysterious Wise Men who traveled a long distance to bring gifts to the Eternal King. In Matthew's Gospel we are told of a group of Star Gazers who find their way to the little town of Bethlehem. Perhaps what is most interesting about this group of people is how mysterious they seem. Some translations call them "kings," some call them "magi," and some simply call them "wise men." We don't know where they come from or how many there are. We only know that "some wise men came from the east, following a star." In this chapter, we will explore the hope that is fulfilled through the Wise Men who visited Jesus.

The Journey of the Wise Men

They been on this journey ever since Jesus was born in Bethlehem, and they first watched his star rise in the sky. They go to pay homage to this new king. Somehow, they seem to know about the birth of this special king. This is pretty remarkable considering that they are foreigners. They are outsiders. They aren't Jewish. Why would Gentiles from the east care anything about the birth of a little Jewish baby in Bethlehem?

Some believe that the Wise Men were probably from an area that is now in either Iraq, Iran, Saudi Arabia, or Yemen. Legends are told about them and old traditions have even given them names: Melchior, Balthazar, and Caspar (or Gaspar).

Melchior wears a gold cloak and has long white hair and a white beard. He is believed to be the king of Persia, and he is remembered as the bearer of the gold that was brought to Jesus.

Balthazar wears a purple cloak and has a black beard. He is believed to be the king of Arabia or sometimes Ethiopia, and he is remembered as the bearer of the myrrh that was brought to Jesus.

Casper wears a green cloak and a gold crown with green jewels in it. He is believed to be the King of India, and he is remembered as the bearer of the frank-incense that was brought to Jesus.[25]

The church where I serve started a new tradition of "chalking the door" on the Twelfth Night, which is the last night of Christmas. Chalking the door is an old tradition from Europe. It is a time where we ask God's blessings to be poured out on our dwellings and upon all who enter our doors. People will often mark their doors at home or the doors of the church with chalk, to celebrate God's blessings for the new year. This tradition is also marked by the arrival of the Wise Men who visited the Christ Child on Epiphany.

Because this night is connected to the visit from the Wise Men, our church decided to have our live nativity on this night as well. On the Twelfth Night, we have folks from the church dress up as Mary, Joseph, and the shepherds. We have a baby doll in the manger representing Jesus. And, of course, we have three people donning fake beards dressed up as the Wise Men. The scene is made complete with a real donkey and calf.

As people gather to witness this scene, they are also encouraged to participate in the chalking of the door. We share in a short liturgy and prayer, and then people are invited to write symbols of the Christian faith in chalk on the sanctuary doors. Some people write a heart, a cross, or a fish. Others write words like "love" or "hope." It is a really special time for people in the church community to offer a blessing for the new year.

One of the time-honored traditions of the chalking of the door is to write the initials C. M. B. in order to symbolize the three Wise Men: Casper, Melchior, and Balthazar. We remember their visit to Jesus and the blessings that they shared through their worship and gifts.

Of course, the names and origins of the Wise Men are all merely speculation. We really don't know who these Wise Men were and where they came from, but it certainly makes for an interesting story. One thing we do know is that the Wise Men are unlikely characters, and they remind us that Jesus is here to break down walls and barriers. Here we see the most mysterious and strange characters brought to the forefront of the Gospel story.

After all, the Wise Men didn't grow up hearing the stories from the prophet Isaiah. They never heard the prophecies of the coming Messiah. They should have no knowledge or context about this newborn king of the Jews, and yet these foreigners, these outsiders, these non-Jews, set themselves on this long and dangerous journey.

Back then, taking a trip wasn't as easy as it is today. They couldn't just jump in their Prius hybrid (that has great gas mileage and can weave between all the transfer trucks on the interstate). They were limited to traveling on foot or riding on a camel or donkey. Which causes us to ask the questions: Why would they make this long and dangerous journey? As a Gentile, why would you leave your comfortable home to go out in search of a Jewish baby?

I think it comes down to one word: believe. They made this journey because they believed. They believed that there was something worth finding. They believed that there was something special about this baby.

Are we not on this same journey? Sometimes we get distracted. Sometimes we forget to look up and search for a star that will take us on a path, on a journey. We sometimes forget to follow the star. Rather than starting out with new goals at the beginning of each year, maybe we can think about this life as a deeper journey. We are invited to travel to Bethlehem. We are invited to believe in Christ, but this journey doesn't always take us on a direct or easy path.

The star did not lead the magi directly to Jesus. The star actually leads them to Jerusalem. This news of Jesus' birth brings some political attention to one person in Jerusalem. King Herod hears about the Wise Men and the birth of this new king, and he is clearly upset. After all, his own title is "King of the Jews." Now the magi are speaking about one who will come to essentially replace him. Herod feels threatened. An old king is worried about the news of a new king that has been born.

King Herod

Herod is certainly a villain. Like Scar, from *The Lion King*, Herod is threatened by a baby cub who is the promised king. Herod is known for having murdered most of his close friends, his wife, and his three sons. He was paranoid and threatened by everyone around him. Emperor Augustus once said that it was safer to be Herod's pig than Herod's son. Perhaps this is because he never felt like he was good enough. He was half Jew and half Idumean. There was Edomite blood in his veins. He didn't come from a pure lineage.[26]

He never felt like he was good enough. Tradition tells us that when he was 70 years old and about to die, he traveled to Jericho and gave the orders that a group of the most distinguished citizens of Jerusalem should be arrested on false charges and imprisoned.

Then he ordered that the moment he died, they should all be killed. He said that he was well aware that no one would mourn his death. He was determined that some tears should be shed when he died - even if the tears weren't mean for him.

This is the kind of figure that Herod was. When he heard about a baby that was born who would replace him, he felt threatened. Then Herod calls a meeting of the leading priests and teachers of religious law. Everyone, along with Herod, is deeply disturbed of this news. Then Herod gathers the same folks who are eventually responsible for Jesus' death on a cross. The religious elite have never been fans of Jesus, even when he was an innocent child. As Matthew's Gospel says:

> *In the time of King Herod, after Jesus was born in Bethlehem of Judea, wise men from the East came to Jerusalem, asking, "Where is the child who has been born king of the Jews? For we observed his star at its rising, and have come to pay him homage." When King Herod heard this, he was frightened, and all Jerusalem with him; and calling together all the chief priests and scribes of the people, he inquired of them where the Messiah was to be born. They told him, "In Bethlehem of Judea; for so it has been written by the prophet:*
>
> *'And you, Bethlehem, in the land of Judah, are by no means least among the rulers of Judah; for from you shall come a ruler who is to shepherd my people Israel."*
>
> —Matthew 2:1-6

They answer Herod's questions, but perhaps they also make up their mind right then and there. Perhaps they decide that this Jesus fellow is just too risky. Matthew doesn't tell us outright, but I have a feeling that, along with Herod, these leading priests and teachers of religious law begin plotting Jesus' death for the first time – a trend that they will continue throughout the Gospels.

Herod calls the Wise Men in for a private meeting, and he sends them on their way to Bethlehem. He gives them the answer they are looking for after consulting the religious leaders, but he attempts to trick them. He says:

> *Go and search diligently for the child; and when you have found him, bring me word so that I may also go and pay him homage.*

—Matthew 2:8

It seems that these Wise Men truly are wise because they see through this ingenuine response. They realize that Herod is trying to play them like a cheap fiddle. The star leads the Wise Men on a path to Bethlehem, and the star leads Herod on a murderous and fearful rampage as he unsuccessfully seeks to kill the Christ Child. The Wise Men cling to the hope that they find in the symbol of the star. They continue to follow the star, believing that it will take them to the promised king.

Gifts of the Wise Men

The Wise Men follow the star to Bethlehem which stops over the place where Jesus was. The Wise Men are filled with joy. The magi come simply to pay homage; they come to worship. They bring the gift of worship along with their gifts of gold, frankincense, and myrrh. Each of these gifts foretell a certain aspect of Jesus' life and ministry.

The first gift that is brought to Jesus is gold. It was customary in that time that when you approached a king you brought him a gift, and gold was considered a gift fit for a king. Jesus has been referred to as the King of kings and Lord of lords, and this gift of gold is a symbol of Jesus' role as king. Jesus was the man born to be king, but he did not function as most people would expect a king to function. Jesus did not reign by force or power or fear. Instead, Jesus reign by grace, love, and hope.

The second gift that is brought to Jesus is the gift of frankincense. Frankincense was used for worship and sacrifices in the Temple. It is a perfume that had a direct connection to the priests. In Jesus' day, the priests had an important job. They were tasked with bridging the gap between man and God. This is exactly what Jesus did. Jesus lives into his role as the great high priest who opens up a way to enter into the presence of God. Jesus comes in the flesh to build a bridge between humanity and God.

The third gift that is brought to Jesus is the gift of myrrh. Myrrh was used in incense as well as in anointing oil. It was often used to embalm dead bodies. The gift of myrrh foreshadows Jesus' death. One of the reasons that Jesus was brought to this world was to come as a living sacrifice. He came into this world to live and die for us, and he was the ultimate sacrifice. This fulfilled the prophecy from Isaiah which says:

A multitude of camels shall cover you, the young camels of Midian and Ephah; all those from Sheba

*shall come. They shall bring gold and frankincense,
and shall proclaim the praise of the Lord.*

—Isaiah 60:6

The gift of gold foretells Jesus' role as a king. The gift of frankincense foretells Jesus' role as a priest. The gift of myrrh foretells of Jesus' death and resurrection. These gifts seem like a strange thing to give a child. Typically, you would give a child diapers, toys, blankets, and pacifiers. However, the gifts of the Wise Men tell us something deeper about Jesus and his time on this earth.

The Wise Men pay homage to the Christ Child, offering him gifts that speak to the kind of king that Jesus would be. These gifts act as prophecies, outlining Jesus' life, ministry, and reign. The Wise Men travel all this way to offer these gifts to Jesus. Then it was time to leave, God warns them in a dream to return to their homes by another route:

*And having been warned in a dream not to return
to Herod, they left for their own country by another
road.*

—Matthew 2:12

It's amazing how much drama this one little baby causes. It really does remind us that Jesus is indeed the Son of God. He has come to shake things up. He has come to remind us that we are not alone, because God is with us. He has come to tell us that we are all invited on this journey. After all, the Wise Men were outsiders, but they were among the first to come and worship Jesus. This story opens the door for the Gentile Christians, for the marginalized, and the outcast; for you and me.

December 21was the longest night of the year in 2020, a year marked by the coronavirus pandemic. It was also the night of a major celestial event called a planetary conjunction. Jupiter and Saturn came so close together that they appeared to be right on top of each other.

With the naked eye, it looked nothing more than just one bright star. With a telescope, however, you could see that the two planets were 0.1 degrees apart, less than the diameter of a full moon. Astronomers marvel at this planetary conjunction, because it is very rare. As Rice University astronomer Patrick Hartigan says:

Alignments between these two planets are rather rare, occurring once every 20 years or so, but this conjunction is exceptionally rare because of how close the planets will appear to one another, you'd have to go all the way back to just before dawn on March 4, 1226, to see a closer alignment between these objects visible in the night sky.[27]

Interestingly, there was an event that took place in the year 2 or 3 BCE when Jupiter, Venus, and Regulus the star were in a planetary conjunction. Therefore, the planetary conjunction is a celestial event which is often nicknamed the "Christmas Star" or the "Star of Bethlehem" because of its possible connection to the story of the Wise Men, who traveled by the light of a great star in the sky.

It is entirely possible that the Wise Men witnessed a planetary conjunction in the sky as a sign of the birth of the Christ Child in Bethlehem. This celestial event paved their way to visit the promised Messiah.

How interesting that on the longest night of the year, there was this miraculous celestial event in the sky. Sometimes in our darkest moments, it is hard to see any sign of light. Sometimes when we find ourselves in the darkness, it is hard to see any hope.

However, in a night when it was the darkest and longest of all the other nights, there was a glimmer of hope in the sky. There was a light shining forth in the darkness. We find hope in this small symbol in the sky. In the Gospel of John, we receive affirmation of this hope:

In the beginning was the Word, and the Word was with God, and the Word was God. He was in the beginning with God. All things came into being through him, and without him not one thing came into being. What has come into being in him was life, and the life was the light of all people. The light shines in the darkness, and the darkness did not overcome it.

—John 1:1-5

In a time when we might feel like we are in a dark place, where the light is shut out from our lives, and we might never see the light again, there is a sign in the sky. The God who created the sun, the moon, and the stars is here among us, guiding us and directing us to join in celebrating God's presence in our promised King. Perhaps we are invited to go out and to do a little star gazing ourselves.

Star Gazing

When I was in college, I would spend my summers working at Camp Lookout, a United Methodist Camp near Chattanooga. On Wednesdays we would have a special night for the middle schoolers called "Camp Out Night."

After a long day of activities, we would eat dinner and then go up to the campfire and roast marshmallows to make smores. The campers would stuff their faces with marshmallows, Hershey's chocolate, and graham crackers.

Once it got dark outside and our eyes had adjusted to the darkness, we would do some stargazing. We had this laser pointer that looked like it was actually reaching up into the sky and touching the stars. It looked like a really long lightsaber that could stretch right up into the galaxy. All the counselors would try to point out one or two stars and constellations that we knew. We would point out the Big Dipper, Little Dipper, Leo, and Arcturus, but that was pretty much the extent of our knowledge in astronomy.

Then we would grab our sleeping bags and pillows, and we would bring them up to this big clearing where we had tarps laid out. Then we would sleep under the stars. It was always a beautiful sight. On clear nights I would have trouble sleeping because it seemed like the stars were so bright. It was almost as if someone had left the lights on.

God of mystery and God of light be with us this day as we journey in our faith and as we worship your Son. Open our hearts so that we can receive your promises of justice and righteousness which are fulfilled in the baby in Bethlehem. Give us courage and hope along our way so that we will continue to follow your path as you guide us in the way you would have us to go. Like the Magi, may you remind us to look up and search for a star to guide us on this Christian journey. And allow us to enter into service and discipleship of your son so that we can tell others of your Good News. Amen.

Reflection Questions

1. The Wise Men traveled several miles to offer gifts of gold, frankincense, and myrrh to the Christ-child. Do you feel like you have had to make a long journey to find Jesus in your life, or do you feel like Jesus has always been close to you?

2. The Wise Men are guided by the light of a star shining in the sky. What are the things that help guide you? Who are the people that have guided you along your journeys in your own life? How might you be a shining star and act as a guide for someone else?

3. How do the gifts of the Wise Men (gold, frankincense, and myrrh) impact your understanding of Jesus as king, priest, and the resurrected Christ? What do these gifts tell us about the kind of ruler Jesus will be?

4. As the Wise Men gave gifts to the Christ Child, how might you offer gifts of hope and peace to others? What are the gifts that you can share with your neighbors, strangers, friends, family, the church, etc.?

5. What is the greatest gift that you have given to someone else? How did giving that gift make you feel?

EPILOGUE

INCARNATION
HOPE MADE FLESH

In the beginning was the Word, and the Word was with God, and the Word was God. He was in the beginning with God. All things came into being through him, and without him not one thing came into being. What has come into being in him was life, and the life was the light of all people. The light shines in the darkness, and the darkness did not overcome it...

And the Word became flesh and lived among us, and we have seen his glory, the glory as of a father's only son, full of grace and truth.
—John 1:1-5; 14

The Christmas story is so crucial because it reminds us that God is not some nebulous being that lives up in the clouds and never interacts with the world. God is not off in the distance, too busy to bother with human beings. Instead, God is a personal God, and God reaches out to us and seeks to work in and around us each and every day. In Eugene Peterson's paraphrase *The Message*, he writes it this way:

> The Word became flesh and blood,
> and moved into the neighborhood.
> —John 1:14 MSG

During Christmas, we celebrate how Jesus enters into life with us. We are told of a Jesus who is present among us through the Incarnation. The term *Incarnation* comes from a Latin word which means "embodiment" or "become flesh." God comes to us in the flesh through the person of Jesus Christ. Each Person of the Trinity: Father, Son, and Holy Spirit, is made of the same substance, and each Person is equal to one another. Athanasius first argued that the Son was of the same substance *(homoousios)*, not merely of similar substance *(homoiousios)* with the Father.[28]

Even in our daily lives, in the mundane things of this world, we still experience the vibrant heart of Jesus beating in and around us. God has given us the greatest gift. In the beginning, there was Jesus, Jesus *the Word*. He was present during the time of creation. The Christian faith is rooted in the understanding that God, who created the stars in the sky, also cares for you and me.

Jesus in Creation

In the very beginning, during the creation of the world, Jesus, the Son, was in existence with God the

Father and God the Spirit. The creation is represented in Scripture:

> *In the beginning God created the heavens and the earth. Now the earth was formless and empty, darkness was over the surface of the deep, and the Spirit of God was hovering over the waters.*
> —Genesis 1:1-12

The Father and the Spirit are both present in the Genesis account of creation. Furthermore, John's Gospel directly indicates that Jesus "was in the beginning with God." Therefore, Christ was present at creation along with the Father and the Holy Spirit. In the beginning, there was Jesus, the Word. He was present during the time of Creation. Jesus is the Word, or as the Greek language states, "The Logos." When God created the heavens and the earth, God did not craft with his hands or wave a magic wand. Instead, God uttered the Word. Remember that God said, "Let there be light, and there was light." God spoke and it came to be, and Jesus was present in that Word.

We see God at the very beginning of creation, forming the cosmos. God created the entire universe, but God also created each one of us. God is a God who knows each one of us intimately, is capable of making the impossible possible, and is eternally present with his people as they experience their earthly lives. Jesus was present in the very beginning along with the Holy Spirit and the Father. Christ was the Word that was made flesh and dwelt among humanity. Jesus came, in the flesh, to share the good news of the kingdom of God, but Christ also revealed himself as the good news itself.

The Word Made Flesh

God has become flesh and moved into the world around us. This is an important reminder to us that words matter. We live in a time where social media is a prime way for people to get their message across.

Everyone has a voice, everyone has an opinion, and it seems that everyone is an expert. We are overloaded with Facebook posts, Tweets, and blogs. We see numerous articles claiming they have all the facts. It has come to a point where words seem like they no longer matter at all. Misinformation is spread, facts are ignored, and conspiracy theories have become mainstream. But the truth is: words do matter.

Words can motivate, encourage, rebuke, and transform. Our words manifest real consequences. I suppose you could say that our words can take on flesh. Sometimes we have a hard time controlling our tongues. I don't know about you, but I have had times in my life where I wished I had kept my mouth shut. I have done some real damage and said some hurtful things. Our words can be used to bless, but they can also be used to curse.

Our kind words to others can encourage and motivate others. Likewise, our negative words can harm and damage others. I was once told that for every negative comment a child hears it takes 7 positive comments to balance it out. Negative words can have a devastating impact on our lives. It can do real and lasting damage. Jesus enters into the world as the Word made flesh, reminding us that the spoken word has power.

The Humanity of Jesus

Jesus enters into this world as a beacon of truth. The great thing about the Christmas story is that Jesus was born into the true reality of this world. Sometimes we forget that Jesus is a real person. Jesus Christ, the Lord, is both fully God and fully man. As Paul writes in his Letter to the Colossians:

> *For in him the whole fullness of deity dwells bodily,*
> *and you have come to fullness in him,*
> *who is the head of every ruler and authority.*
> —Colossians 2:9,10

Jesus experienced the fullness of human emotion. Throughout the Gospels we see Jesus grow tired, hungry, and thirsty. We see him being tempted in the wilderness. We see him get angry, and we see him feel sad and weep. We see him become physically weak while carrying the cross. We see him beaten and bloody, and we see him die on the cross.

Jesus came fully in human form to enter into our lives and deal with our struggles, sins, and mistakes. That is what the story of Christmas is all about. Christmas is about God's response to our ugliness, to our sin, and to our brokenness. God comes and brings us hope. In his humanness, we can connect to Jesus. However, Jesus is not only fully human, but he is also divine. We see hope radiate beyond his death and through his resurrection. Jesus continues to bring light into the world.

In his book *Night*, Elie Wiesel writes about his experience in the Auschwitz concentration camp. This German Nazi camp is the place where both his parents and his sister died. It is the place where he personally witnessed unspeakable horrors. He told of one terrible evening when the whole camp was forced to witness the hanging of three prisoners. One of them was just a child whose crime was stealing bread. Wiesel deemed the young boy "the sad-eyed angel." The two men died instantly at the hanging, but the young boy was too light; he was still breathing. Wiesel writes about this episode saying:

> And so he remained for more than half an hour, lingering between life and death, writhing before our eyes. And we were forced to look at him at close range. He was still alive when I passed him. His tongue was still red, his eyes not yet extinguished. Behind me, I heard the same man asking:

> "For God's sake, where is God?"

> And from within me, I heard a voice answer:
> "Where is He? This is where – hanging from the gallows."[29]

There are times when we might feel as if God is nowhere to be found. There are times when we might feel as if we are all alone without anyone in the world. There are times when we might feel as if nobody understands who we are and the things we are going through. When you are experiencing the loss of a loved one; when your spouse is battling a terminal illness; when you are fighting feelings of depression and loneliness – these are times when it can be hard to see any glimmer of light.

The Light of Christ

When the world looks like it can't get any darker, God comes and brings a light into our dark world. Light is something that we often take for granted. I want you to think about the last time your power went out. It is a huge inconvenience. You have to search for candles or flashlights. You look around in order to find a source of light so that you can see in the darkness.

I think we forget how often we are stumbling around in the dark. I think we forget how often we are led astray. Jesus has come to bring light to the situation. He brings light in order to show us where we may need help. He brings light to show us the right way to go. Jesus has come as a light into this world. Jesus has come to live among us. Jesus is here with us now, and he offers us an invitation to accept him into our hearts.

In the coming of Jesus, we find redemption. In the coming of Jesus, we find that we are not alone. In Jesus, we see God with us: walking with us, talking to us, guiding us, teaching us, forgiving us, weeping with us, laughing with us, and raising us. It's incredible that in our pain and in our suffering, the God of the Universe is here among us. In our broken lives and in our broken world, God is with us. God entered into this place and came among us in the flesh.

As we reflect on God's presence with us, we are invited to think about how we can be present in other people's lives. How might we reach out to the people in our neighborhood? How might we find ways to share God's love through the way we interact with others? How can we move into people's neighborhoods and share in people's lives? This Christmas season, how might we offer God's love to others? I'm reminded of a hymn that calls us to follow in the light of Christ. It says:

I want to walk as a child of the light
I want to follow Jesus
God sent the stars to give light to the world
The star of my life is Jesus

In Him, there is no darkness at all
The night and the day are both alike
The Lamb is the light of the city of God
Shine in my heart, Lord Jesus

I want to see the brightness of God
I want to look at Jesus

Clear sun of righteousness, shine on my path
And show me the way to the Father

In Him, there is no darkness at all
The night and the day are both alike
The Lamb is the light of the city of God
Shine in my heart, Lord Jesus[30]

The presence of God in our world shows us that God's love is infinite – it just is. God offers God's love to us, and we are called to go out and love our neighbor as we love ourselves. Jesus came to bring light into this world, and we have a responsibility to take that light and share it with others. We are called to make disciples of Jesus Christ for the transformation of the world! We are called to share the hope that we find in the holidays with others. We are called to walk as a child of the light. Jesus, who came as a baby in the manger, has come to bring hope to the whole world.

Christmas Eve Candlelight

One of my favorite memories growing up in my home church, First United Methodist in Cleveland, Tennessee, is the Christmas Eve candlelight service. Each year, on Christmas Eve, I would walk into the sanctuary, and I would notice how bright it seemed compared to the darkness and the cold of the outside. I was rarely in the sanctuary during the evening, so I was seeing the sanctuary in a special way.

My parents, sister, and I would sit in our regular pew – the pew that we sat in every single Sunday. I would look around at all the people and familiar faces that I had known since my birth. I was surrounded by people whom I loved and the people who loved me. In that space, I felt safe and secure. I felt as if I was at home.

Together, the congregation would sing some of my favorite Christmas hymns, we would hear a sermon, and then we would share in Holy Communion. Finally, at the end of the service, the congregation would join in singing a Christmas hymn. The ushers had handed out candles to each individual at the beginning of the service and, during this hymn, they would walk by each pew lighting candles. Slowly the lights in the sanctuary were dimmed until eventually the only light available in the room came from each individual's candle. Lights shining in the darkness. It is in moments like this that I have experienced God's hope in my own life in the most profound ways.

God of infinite love, we thank you for your constant presence in our lives, we don't always feel your presence as much as we would like, but you are always with us. We thank you for the gift of love you have offered to us through your Son, Jesus Christ. Fill us with your hope, peace, and love during the Christmas Season. May we listen to your call to love you and our neigh-

bors. May we go forth as we strive to make disciples of your Son. Amen.

ABOUT
KHARIS PUBLISHING

KHARIS PUBLISHING is an independent, traditional publishing house with a core mission to publish impactful books, and channel proceeds into establishing mini-libraries or resource centers for orphanages in developing countries, so these kids will learn to read, dream, and grow. Every time you purchase a book from Kharis Publishing or partner as an author, you are helping give these kids an amazing opportunity to read, dream, and grow. Kharis Publishing is an imprint of Kharis Media LLC. Learn more at https://www.kharispublishing.com.

ABOUT THE AUTHOR

Rev. Andrew Curtis Lay is a native of Cleveland, Tennessee. He is a life-long Methodist and grew up attending First United Methodist Church in Cleveland. He earned his bachelor's degree at Tennessee Wesleyan University, where he has also taught as an adjunct professor in the religion department. He also completed his Master of Divinity degree at Asbury Theological Seminary. In June 2019, he was commissioned as a provisional member in the Holston Conference of the United Methodist Church, and he is now in the process of seeking ordination.

Andrew is currently serving as the associate pastor of Keith Memorial United Methodist Church in Athens, Tennessee. He and his wife, Ally, have a passion for music, ministry, and the outdoors. Furthermore, Andrew has a love for God and for the mission of the United Methodist Church, which is "to make disciples of Jesus Christ for the transformation of the world."

CITED WORK

1. Ronald J. Allen, Dale P. Andrews, and Dawn Ottoni-Wilhelm, eds., *Preaching God's Transforming Justice: A Lectionary Commentary, Year C* (Louisville, KY: Westminster John Knox Press, 2012).

2. Walter Bauer and Frederick W. Danker, *A Greek-English Lexicon of the New Testament and Other Early Christian Literature:* (Chicago, IL: Univ. of Chicago Press, 2000).

3. John Wesley and Kenneth J. Collins, *The Sermons of John Wesley: A Collection for the Christian Journey* (Nashville, TN: Abingdon Press, 2013), 137.

4. William H. Willimon, *Will Willimon's Lectionary Sermon Resource, Year C., Part 1* (Nashville, TN: Abingdon, 2018), 11.

5. Cynthia A. Jarvis and E. Elizabeth Johnson, *Feasting on the Gospels. a Feasting on the Word Commentary*, Luke Volume 1 (Louisville, KY: Westminster John Knox Press, 2014).

6. Susan Beaumont, *How to Lead When You Don't Know Where You're Going: Leading in a Liminal Season* (Lanham, MD: Rowman & Littlefield, 2019).

7. Foo Fighters. *Times Like These*. Foo Fighters, 2003.

8. Adam Hamilton, *Faithful: Christmas through the Eyes of Joseph* (Nashville, TN: Abingdon Press, 2017), 50.

9. Leander E. Keck, *The New Interpreter's Bible Commentary*, VII (Nashville: Abingdon Press, 2015), 71.

10. John Wesley, *The Heart of John Wesley's Journal*, ed. Percy Livingston. Parker (Peabody, MA: Hendrickson, 2008), 526, 527.

11. Doug Gresham, "Remembering My Stepdad: Reflections from C. S. Lewis's Stepson," *Official Site | CSLewis.com*, last modified March 9, 2014, accessed December 9, 2020, https://www.cslewis.com/remembering-my-stepdad-reflections-from-c-s-lewiss-stepson/.

12. Adam Hamilton, *Faithful: Christmas through the Eyes of Joseph* (Nashville, TN: Abingdon Press, 2017), 11.

13. Francesca Battistelli, Nichole Nordeman, and Bernhard Herms. *Be Born in Me (Mary)*. EMI CMG/Word/Provident, MP3, 2011.

14. Martin Luther, "Works of Martin Luther Volume 3," *The Ages Digital Library Collections* (1997), accessed December 14, 2020, 117.

15. William H. Willimon, *Why Jesus?* (Nashville: Abingdon Press, 2010), 61.

16. "Can We Feed the World and Ensure No One Goes Hungry? | | UN News," *United Nations* (United Nations, October 3, 2019), last modified October 3, 2019, accessedJanuary 28, 2021, https://news.un.org/en/story/2019/10/1048452.

17. Annette Spence, "Holston Grant Provides Face Masks for 2,500 in East Africa," *The Call, the Holston Conference Newspaper.* (December 10, 2020), accessed December 14, 2020,

https://www.holston.org/article/masks-sanitizers-gloves-for-uganda-14856834.

18. Steve Martin and the Steep Canyon Rangers. *The Strangest Christmas Yet*. MP3. *The Long-Awaited Album*, 2017.

19. John Lewis and Partners. "The Boy and the Piano." YouTube, 2018. Accessed December 22, 2020, https://www.youtube.com/watch?time_continue=7&v=GRG14lyjtw4&feature=emb_title.

20. Adam Hamilton, *The Journey: Walking the Road to Bethlehem* (Nashville, TN: Abingdon Press, 2016).

21. Susan Lewis, "The Story Behind the Beloved Christmas Carol 'Silent Night,'" *WRTI*, last modified December 16, 2020, accessed December 22, 2020, https://www.wrti.org/post/story-behind-beloved-christmas-carol-silent-night.

22. *The United Methodist Hymnal Book of United Methodist Worship* (Nashville, TN: The United Methodist Publishing House, 2001), 239.

23. Christopher Klein, "World War I's Christmas Truce," *History.com* (A&E Television Networks, December 19, 2014), last modified December 19, 2014, accessed December 22, 2020, https://www.history.com/news/world-war-is-christmas-truce-100-years-ago.

24. *The Lion King* (Walt Disney Home Entertainment, 2003).

25. "Magi," *Encyclopædia Britannica* (Encyclopædia Britannica, inc., December 9, 2020), last modified December 9, 2020, accessed January 28, 2021, https://www.britannica.com/topic/Magi.

26. Leonard J. Greenspoon, "Herod the Great." *Salem Press Biographical Encyclopedia*.

27. Sophie Lewis, "Jupiter and Saturn Will Come within 0.1 Degrees of Each Other, Forming the First Visible 'Double Planet' in 800 Years," *CBS News* (CBS Interactive, December 21, 2020), last modified December 21, 2020, accessed December 23, 2020, https://www.cbsnews.com/news/saturn-jupiter-winter-solstice-great-conjunction/.

28. William C. Placher, *Readings in the History of Christian Theology*. Vol. 1. 2 vols. (Philadelphia, PA: Westminster John Knox Press, 1988), 48.

29. Elie Wiesel, *Night: Elie Wiesel* (New York, NY: Spark Publishing, 2014).

30. *The United Methodist Hymnal Book of United Methodist Worship* (Nashville, TN: The United Methodist Publishing House, 2001), 206.

CPSIA information can be obtained
at www.ICGtesting.com
Printed in the USA
LVHW080215140821
695215LV00003B/22

9 781637 460283